M·C·A

MANAGEMENT
CONSULTANCIES
ASSOCIATION

Series Editor: Fiona Czerniawska, Director of MCA Think Tank.

The MCA was formed in 1956 and represents the leading UK-based consulting firms, which currently employ over 25,000 consultants and generate £4.3bn in annual fee income. The UK consulting industry is worth around £8bn, contributing £1bn to the balance of payments.

As well as setting and maintaining standards in the industry, the MCA supports its member firms with a range of services including events, publications, interest groups and public relations. The Association also works with its members to attract the top talent into the industry. The MCA provides advice on the selection and use of management consultants and is the main source of data on the UK market.

FOR MORE INFORMATION PLEASE CONTACT:
Management Consultancies Association
49 Whitehall
London
SW1A 2BX

Tel: 020 7321 3990
Fax: 020 7321 3991

E-mail: mca@mca.org.uk
www.mca.org.uk

CONTENTS

ACKNOWLEDGEMENTS

To the clients of the Axon Group; who provided much of the insight, learning and practical examples upon which this book is based.

And to Louise, for helping me out yet again!

FOREWORD

The e-business revolution, which gripped the corporate world during the end of the last millennium and the beginning of this one, is responsible for many things. Well-known corporations made inappropriate and substantive investments in things they did not understand. Firms that should never have started trading were lent vast sums by naïve professional and private investors. High levels of corporate risks, never seen before, were taken, often unwittingly.

However, this period of brief hysteria did bring to the surface powerful but untapped business tools. Collaboration was one of these trading phenomenons. Since the Industrial Revolution, with a few notable exceptions, firms had focused on how they could improve their own operations. Collaboration opened up a new door – the gateway to industry transformation. The ultimate prize would no longer be about winners and losers in a particular sector or market – but the performance of industries as a whole.

In this book, Stephen Cardell, a fellow Director and head of Bywater, Axon's Business Consulting Division, takes us forward to the potential benefits of fully networked industries, and back to the fundamentals of how collaborative ventures should be structured, operated and managed. The value of this book to business people everywhere is that it offers the kind of practical applications needed in today's competitive marketplace. Accessing the resources of not just your own organization, but those of others, will be the key to success.

Mark Hunter
Founder and Chief Executive
Axon Group Plc.

INTRODUCTION

THE COLLABORATION CHALLENGE

Strategic context

The mobile telecommunications company, Orange, has regularly won awards, which recognize the unique lifestyle brand that has powered its growth. Yet it was a UK City branding firm, not Orange, who actually developed and implemented their marketplace presence. In a similar fashion, GlaxoSmithKline (gsk) dominates the life sciences sector with blockbuster drugs, even though many of these patented giants were initially conceived by small R&D (research and development) houses, not gsk itself. Intel has sown up the marketplace for PC processing, although it controls no retail outlets, value-added resellers (VARs) or direct channels to the consumer marketplace. Indeed, for many of the world's most successful corporations, the very things that have made them great are neither developed nor owned in-house. They have been achieved through collaborative relationships.

The concept of collaboration is commonly recognized to have been originally developed by the Japanese *keiretsu* (conglomerate). Here, cross-company relationships within the large trading families replaced the need for legal ownership. When the West caught on, the term 'partnership' was initially used to describe the recognized need for traditional supply chain providers to operate with one another in a more win-win and less confrontational manner. As the benefits of this approach become apparent, the term 'alliancing' emerged for relationships that became more strategic in nature. Today, with whole industry sectors such as oil, airlines, automotive, aerospace and telecommunications dependent on supplier-provider relationships to deliver their marketplace promise, collaboration has become a more appropriate term to describe this rapidly growing phenomenon.

Critical importance

GartnerGroup predict that for the average company, 65 per cent of total supply chain costs will be delivered by providers outside the firm's borders by 2005. In a world where BP has oil platforms it does not operate, Vodafone has networks it does not own and Ford has car plants it did not build, collaborative relationships are becoming the critical component for business success in the twenty-first century.

To provide a guide for organizations embarking upon the collaboration path, this book is dedicated to answering four key questions:

1   When is a collaborative relationship appropriate?

2   What types of collaborate relationship models exist?

3   How do you create and operate collaborate relationships?

4   How do collaborative companies differ from traditional ones?

This book will provide a structure and approach for either executives tasked with defining whether a collaborate relationship is the appropriate model to use in a particular situation, or for managers who are attempting to make collaborative aspirations a reality. The book is broken into four main parts, which cover identifying the need, models of collaboration, operating collaborative relationships and managing in the networked economy. In a final summary chapter the key issues, questions and challenges of each section are covered.

A ROUTE MAP FOR COLLABORATION

Part 1: Defining the need

Choosing collaborative approaches – Much confusion surrounds both the need to collaborate and the definition of collaboration. In part, this is due to the overuse of the word to describe electronic trading relationships during dot.com mania. Whether the basis of transacting a relationship is electronic or physical, this is a poor indicator of its level of strategic importance.

Quite simply, organizations should consider a collaborative relationship if two criteria can be met:

1   Is the business objective, which the collaborative relationship would deliver, strategic?

2   Are there external parties with greater resources, capabilities or market power that could enable the business goal to be delivered more easily?

Collaborative relationships is only one model along the continuum of possible company-to-company interactions. The first step for success is to ensure that the scope of activity considered for such a relationship level is appropriate.

Collaboration approaches may be used to achieve very different ends, and it is critical to understand the rationale and purpose of an engagement. The reasons that General Motors collaborates with its tier 1 suppliers (i.e. its most strategic suppliers only who then manage the less important suppliers) in the automotive value chain are quite different to why BAe entered into the four-company collaboration to create the Eurofighter project, which was formed to enable Europe to compete with the American defense industry. The founding members of the Star Alliance in the airline sector had a very different game plan to Shell, when Shell created a six-company collaboration to more effectively operate oil platforms off the coast of Mexico.

In principle, there are four strategic models of cross-company collaboration, which exist to achieve fundamentally different strategic outcomes. In some instances, the same company-to-company relationship can be used to achieve more than one of these goals, but if that is the case, there are entirely different facets to that corporate relationship. These four models are:

1   **Supply chain collaboration** – Which recognizes that delivery of the firms' products or services to the end customer is more effectively achieved when strategic suppliers and customers are managed in a collaborative manner.

2   **Capability-based collaboration** – Where skills or competencies necessary to deliver an organization's strategy are provided by a third party.

3 **Proposition-based collaboration** – Where the desired product or service offering to the customer community can only be achieved through the combined resources of two or more organizations.

4 **Competitive collaboration** – Which uses the exchange of Porterian[1] market power as the basis for mutual benefit.

For completeness, there is a fifth model of collaboration, which takes us right back to the Japanese *keiretsu*. Here, collaborative techniques are used in a situation where merger is the desired legal relationship, but where this is impossible because of speed, legal barriers or corporate desire. This quasi-collaborative approach, while offering its own set of insights and challenges, is not the topic of this book.

CHARACTERISTICS	SUPPLY CHAIN	CAPABILITY	PROPOSITION	COMPETITIVE
SCOPE OF ACTIVITY	Same scope as pre-collaboration	Same scope as pre-collaboration	Increased	Same or increased
FOCUS OF COLLABORATION	Cost	Skills	Market offer	Power
TYPICAL NUMBER OF PARTIES	Two or three	Two	Two → Many	Two → Many
RISK OF FAILURE	Low	Medium	High	High
IMPORTANCE OF CULTURE FIT	High	Medium	Medium	Low

TABLE 1: Models of collaboration

Part 2: Four models of collaboration

Supply chain collaboration – This developed out of the desire to eradicate non-added value activities. Within an organization, the greatest cause of error and re-work exists at the boundary between departments. Each checking the other's work; both planning on behalf of the other. A detailed survey of the cause of error and re-work from 24 companies found that around 47 per cent was caused by problems at these departmental interfaces.

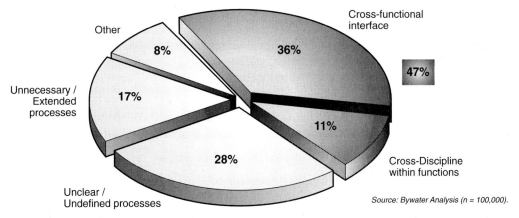

FIGURE 1: Causes of error and re-work within organizations

[1] This is based on Michael Porter's *Five Forces Model* which looks at the five inherent drivers of power in an industry; supplier power, buyer power, barriers to entry, threat of substitutes and rivalry.

Now imagine that it is companies, not departments. The amount of checking, negotiating and duplicating of effort rises exponentially. And for what value? An analysis of one supply chain concluded that over 30 per cent of the activities undertaken from raw material supplier, fabricator and assembler, to end customer added no value to the end product. These activities could then be eliminated with no loss to any party.

Take Ford and VW as a radical example of this. Both companies are in an industry that has often led the development of supply chain collaboration through the evolution of tiered supply communities and lean supply. Recently, Ford and VW recognized that they were both losing economies of scale in the production of their people carrier models – the Galaxy and Sharan. While fiercely competitive in the consumer marketplace, Ford and VW signed up to a 'co-makership' agreement. Under this arrangement, both models are made on the same production line, with mostly the same component parts. Ford and VW employees sit together in production planning meetings, and then release finished goods that go head to head once they hit the dealer network. Yet, what is clear is that both firms have seen their unit cost base reduce dramatically. So, supply chain collaboration is not just about operating more effectively with your strategic suppliers, it can involve partnering with your competitors, and competing with your partners.

Capability-based collaboration – Let us return to Orange. When Hans Snook, the founding chief executive of Orange, developed the concept of Orange as a lifestyle brand, he had the vision within his firm, but not the ability to execute this cornerstone of the company's success. What he required was a partner who could bring the design and implementation skills which he had neither the time nor desire to build in-house. He needed a provider he could collaborate with – one that had the capability to make this strategic aspiration a reality.

Collaborating to acquire capability does not increase the overall scope of activities conducted by the organization – it may simply use partners for some of the existing activities in a more effective way. The early examples of capabilities provided by third parties were in the initial days of outsourcing. This typically involved non-strategic areas, such as payroll processing, application support or facilities management. While these were capabilities acquired externally, they did not warrant a collaborative relationship with the provider because they were not strategic, and switching costs were low. However, more recently, firms have begun to recognize that even areas, which are seen as core, can be better provided by external organizations, for example, Roche outsourcing R&D, or Coca-Cola outsourcing the physical production of their legendary product.

The starting point for any assessment of potential collaboration in this area is first and foremost an understanding of the organization's core competence, which is required to achieve the business goals. Developed by Gary Hamel and C K Prahlahaad in the mid 1980s, core competence is a well-tried and tested path that can set the agenda for a review of potential collaboration areas.

Proposition-based collaboration – What makes proposition-based collaboration unique from other forms, is that the outcome of the relationship leads to a new product or service offering for the customer community. To be precise, it expands the scope of activities of the organizations participating in the collaborative relationship. At its simplest level this form of collaboration involves two firms bundling their services together to make a new offer, for instance, McDonald's and Walt Disney create themed meal time experiences, or TimeWarner and AOL provide the only route of access and delivery to one of the greatest video libraries on the planet.

However, proposition collaboration can go much further than simply adding one and one together to make a new customer offer. Novartis brought together their seeds business, historically developed by Sandoz, with their crop protection business. Rather than farmers sowing seed and spraying insecticide when the plants were grown, a new product was developed where the protection was built into the seed – avoiding huge costs in the agriculture value chain, and completely differentiating the Novartis offer.

Proposition-based collaboration is the most common model which precedes a move to the next step in the relationship continuum – to a merger or acquisition. Moreover, for many companies it is a good step to consider if merger is the likely outcome because it tests the organizations' ability to work together.

Cisco Systems is a tremendous example; almost their entire market offering was created through proposition-based collaboration, which often later turned to acquisition. In the last ten years, over 300 companies have helped Cisco to create the market dominant position that it holds today.

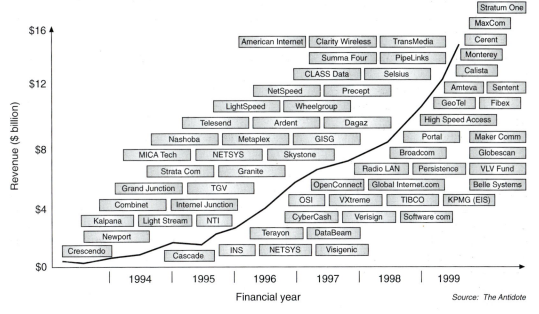

FIGURE 2: Cisco Systems collaborative and acquisitive past

Competitive collaboration – Have the best products and services, and you can win in the marketplace. Offer better customer service, and growth will come. However, this is not the only way: dominate the route to the customer and take out the ability to compete on traditional grounds. And what better way to do that than through collaborative relationships?

Fly Emirates airlines and the car hire service, if you need one, will be Budget. Does the customer have a choice? Not really. Do they want one? Not if it is all taken care of by Emirates. Budget have collaborated with Emirates; Emirates have sole access to their on-board customers, and by working together with Budget, market power has displaced the traditional levers of competition.

It is the same when you gain points at BP, which can only be used on Argos products, or buy financial services products at Tesco, which are only provided by Royal Bank of Scotland. Often the company providing the service is invisible to the purchasing consumer and yet a channel to market has been sown up by a provider.

Part 3: Operating collaborative relationships

Collaboration establishment – Deciding whether to collaborate, and which model is appropriate is the simple part. More difficult is to make the relationship between two or more parties deliver the goals that are expected. Firms often struggle to facilitate different functions within the same company in order to work together effectively – let alone where those relationships cross corporate and often country boundaries.

Taking a step-by-step approach to the identification, development and management of a collaborative relationship is the starting point to ensure that the journey can be traversed effectively. While there are a number of steps in this process, four are critical for the goals to be achieved:

1 Choosing the right business partner or partners with whom to embark on the collaboration journey.

2 Creating shared goals and values between the organizations involved.

3 Putting in place an integrated planning process to support the achievement of business goals.

4 Establishing a common measurement model as the basis for ongoing performance management.

Partner selection – In 1992, General Motors Corporation made headlines by demanding double-digit price cuts from its strategic suppliers, by breaking long-term contracts and by sharing information with rivals in a quest for lower bids. The company focused on price with its suppliers alone – it ignored total costs. In the end, General Motors polarized its partners and lost market share.

The challenge of collaborating with external organizations has led to two commonly used definitions of the word collaboration, which in turn demonstrate the fundamental challenge of partner selection. These definitions for collaboration are:

1 Working together with a strategic partner for mutual gain.

2 Willingly assisting the enemy.

As one global US-owned corporation recently commented, 'We don't do collaboration any more – we never get the benefits we know are there. If they're strategic we buy them'.

A recent assessment that evaluated the critical success factors for cross-company collaboration found that a clearly identified and understood business need for going down this route was the single most important factor.

How can you know if the partner you choose will help you to join the first definition of collaboration described earlier, and not put you into the camp of willingly assisting the enemy? The critical test is to recognize the prerequisites needed between two or more firms which are attempting to create business value together, and to assess whether those required ingredients are in place, and are able to set the foundation for success.

Shared goals and values – Collaboration is about shared pain to deliver shared gain. Therefore, before the pain begins, a foundation of shared goals and shared values is an

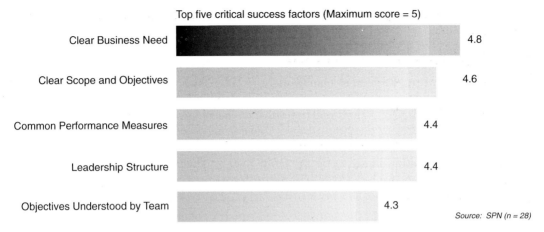

FIGURE 3: Critical success factors for collaboration success

absolute critical starting point. There are many ways to develop the shared goals – the approach to any of the party's strategic planning process could be used. However, the single most important test of those stated goals is that they fully align back to the goals of the individual organizations.

By asking each participating organization to write on a single sheet of paper their objectives and critical success factors (for the company, not the collaboration), you have created the checklist to ensure goal congruence. If the two statements of purpose are then brought together, areas of common interest and conflict can be identified. From this basis, a set of truly aligned goals can be developed for the collaboration, to lead to concrete targets.

Shared values is a topic which all too often goes on the 'too difficult' pile, and yet it is probably the greatest single reason why collaborative relationships do not deliver the value they should. A cultural assessment is a good place to start. If an entrepreneurial firm is trying to tango with a hierarchical company doing the foxtrot, it is good to know that from the start.

Integrated planning – If you know where you want to go with the collaboration – the shared goals – the planning involves saying what you will do to get you there. It has two elements:

1 **Known problems (incremental change)** – Involves listing all the known areas of difficulty or problems, and defining what would be needed by all parties to put these problems right.

2 **Unconstrained opportunities (step changes)** – For example, the supplier who moves their factory and puts it next to the customer. Or the customer that bases quality assurance staff at the supplier's factory. Or where the R&D departments of two firms are merged together. These are the 'out of the box' ideas.

It is important that the planning process is open, done jointly, and that known problems and unconstrained opportunities are discussed separately. If not, the debate quickly reverts to the known, rather than searching for the greater potential of the unknown.

What sort of improvements are possible? Typical areas which need to be reviewed in the planning process include processes, technology, skills and capabilities, structure and governance, relationships and management and reporting.

Collaboration, like any change program, needs early wins to convince both parties that this was a good route to go down. Prioritizing the opportunities identified by the planning process, and using that as the basis to set out a joint action plan, ensures that some of the 'low-hanging fruit' is picked first, before setting off up Mount Everest together.

Measurement and performance management – If measures are the glue that holds organizations together, then their importance when dealing with multiple companies is even greater. When shared goals, values and actions have been agreed, the only way to keep the collaboration on track is to measure progress towards them. However, the construction of a measures model for a collaboration is subtly different to that of a company. The purpose of a particular collaboration tends to be far more focused than that of a company. Where a balanced scorecard approach is extremely useful for firms, and can be equally applied to a collaboration context, focus is the key word.

Take an R&D collaboration in the aerospace industry. It exists to design a new plane within a certain cost and time frame. Period. Or a topside (i.e. all equipment held above the water line) collaboration in the oil industry. Its primary aim is maximum production (topside efficiency) for minimum operating cost. That is it. The operator of that oil platform may have many other considerations. And they have the whole asset to think about, not just topside. However, for the specific collaborative relationships, it is the two strategic measures of production and cost that matter.

Hence, a cascade measures model, which is driven from the two or three strategic measures that define the purpose of the collaboration, is often most effective. Lower level measures that link root cause elements to the strategic goals are the order of the day. Therefore, keeping the whole thing simple and focused is the key to success. It is also essential that all parties view these measures in the same way from the same data.

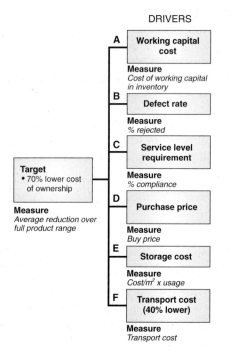

FIGURE 4: Example of a deployed measures model

Part 4: Managing in the networked economy

Creating networked companies – There are already members of the FTSE (Financial Times Stock Exchange) and Fortune 100 companies who source more than 50 per cent of the value of their sales from external partners, not from resources owned by their own corporation. If this trend continues, the concept of the networked economy truly begins to shift into the arena of real business. When dot.com mania was gripping the business world, many claimed the networked economy was already here – somewhat prematurely. However, the snapshot of that wave of change is significant in its ramification. Amazon.com, whether history will ultimately decide it a success or failure, can claim to have built a global brand. It is a multi-billion dollar corporation and the largest bookseller on the planet, through broadly owning nothing. This took six months from concept to implementation. Collaborative partners built the whole thing – Amazon itself owned virtually nothing – and so it was with most of the dot.coms. Moreover, when one looks further afield it is not so different. AT&T, the telecommunications giant, operates a complete communication service in 149 countries, but only owns proprietary networks in a handful. In the UK, the four mobile giants of Orange, O2, Vodafone and T-mobile spent four years and over $2 billion each building a Global System for Mobile Communications (GSM) network – and then Virgin mobile went from launch to profit in six months, owning nothing but the headed paper.

So, where is this leading? What are the critical aspects to consider as we live increasingly in the networked economy where collaborative ventures, not legal entities, deliver the marketplace promise? In short, there are three things to consider:

1   Recognize the two fundamental competencies that the organization must retain: strategy development and partner management.

2   Create an effective process to evolve collaborative relationships – either towards acquisition or out of existence, as the company strategy changes.

3   Have absolute clarity about which cards to play at the industry level where power is exchanged not in horizontal competitive games, but along vertical monopolies.

Strategy and partner management – The Dilbert Series, written by Scott Adamson, while poking fun at corporate incompetence, is an example itself of the brave new world. The Dilbert brand generates tens of millions of dollars in sales each year, sells to over 40 countries, and yet is managed by Scott Adamson and a couple of colleagues. How? Because everything in the Dilbert value chain, from journalists, publishers, distributors, website designers and accounting is done via partners. Adamson, after all, would not profess to have any great expertise in any of these areas. He controls only two things – the Dilbert copyright and material, and the legal contracts with all the partners. In other words, he has the strategy and he manages collaborative relationships. Furthermore, it could be like this with a multi-billion dollar corporation.

Shared services in their entirety could go to an integrated business process outsourcing (BPO) firm like eXchanging, taking out finance, HR (Human Resources) and the rest of the back office in one go. All IT (Information Technology) could go to IBM. The billing and call centres could be managed by Vertex, a company set up by United Utilities, initially as an internal BPO for all their back office services. Infrastructure and operations could be given to Amey, another BPO service business that operates globally. Marketing can go to an agency, all the office buildings to one of the Facilities Management (FM) giants like Haden or Mowlems, and even investor relations to a firm of analysts far more focused on the needs of the stakeholders.

In fact, depending on the organization, just about anything could be done through a third-party relationship; everything apart from two elements.

Firstly, strategy has to remain the domain of the company. Orange may have collaborated to build the brand, and gsk to create its drugs, but the strategy and aspiration of what was needed had to remain in-house. It is the DNA of the company – the factor that makes it unique. And secondly, the competence to effectively manage collaborative partners is, and will be increasingly, the other key factor. If Hans Snook at Orange had been unable to manage his key partner, the dream would never have become a reality. Managing collaborative partners must cover everything from legal relationships, to the creation and management of shared goals and values.

Relationship evolution – Once you have started down the road of a collaborative relationship, is that it? Like any other form of business-to-business relationship, collaboration needs to be monitored from a strategic and operational standpoint. This is in order to understand whether the area of scope still warrants a collaborative model, and also whether the partner or partners chosen are delivering the promise. Sometimes, the collaboration works so well that an acquisition is the logical and right answer. Once Lloyds bank realized that its collaborative relationship with Abbey Life was creating a new marketplace proposition to the consumer base in 1989 – 'bancassurance' – it could no longer leave its unique differentiator in the hands of a partner. Acquisition was the logical answer, and indeed a strategic imperative.

Conversely, the joint shop proposition that Marks & Spencer and Tesco trialled together, while partially successful, began to clash. Both firms' independent strategies moved into each other's product space and the collaboration had to be dismantled. Its ongoing existence would have provided a strategic conflict that could not be permitted to continue.

Therefore, although the engagement of a collaborative relationship by definition has a high cost of exit, it is not a relationship model that can be set in stone. Its appropriateness to the strategy of the firm must be an ongoing point of review.

Vertical monopolies – Let us take the retail food industry as a case in point. Automotive production and PC manufacturing would also demonstrate the issue well. Two online internet exchange companies have emerged on the scene, where the retail giants like Wal-Mart, Tesco, Sainsbury's and Peacocks attempt to drive consolidated buyer power and industry standardization. Two camps have formed – one called GlobalNetXchange (GNX), and the other WorldWide Retail Exchange (WWRE), with each of the major players deciding which one to join. This is reminiscent of the Star and OneWorld Alliances in the airline industry. Immediately the collaborative decision of which company to join belongs fairly and squarely on the chief executive's table, and it has nothing to do with cost, quality or service. It is about two horses leaving the starting blocks, and companies making a business-busting gamble on which one is going to win.

The two competing retail exchanges are each trying to sign up the major suppliers – Coca-Cola, Kellogg's, Heinz and the like. Should these firms join both, or do they become enticed by the offers and pick just one, and go double or quits? This could be the beginning of a vertical monopoly. Coca-Cola has already sole-sourced its can manufacturers and bottling plants – the whole value chain from mining steel to selling a can of coke could become a single route track. No competition, no choice – a monopoly. The monopoly will not extend to the end-user market because traditional industries have been defined, and competition commission auditors focus their attention along the value chain from tertiary industry providers to the final consumer.

In the case of retail, the major suppliers see the competing retail exchanges as meaning only one thing – power slipping further towards the supermarkets. Transora has now entered the arena and is the exchange controlled by the supplier community, dwarfing both the retailer-led offerings. It may have been set-up to improve service, but this is certainly not the only reason.

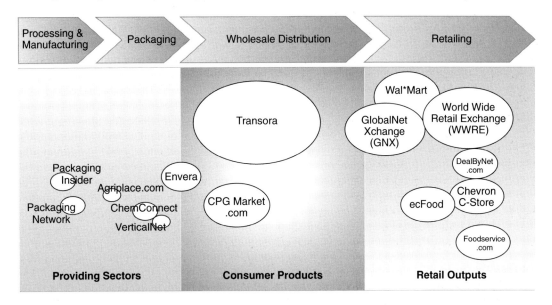

FIGURE 5: The networked economy for the retail sector

Porterian power games are being played and the collaborative relationships are not about two partners coming together to shave 5 per cent off the supply chain costs. They are more to do with executives gambling with the future of their companies when collaboration replaces merger and acquisition. Partners are no longer players in your traditional space, but they are the access point to new and innovative markets.

Conclusions

Collaboration should be, and must be, critical in the growth aspirations of any corporation. In a business world where no firm can build capability quickly or cheaply enough to win, accessing resources, innovation and geographic presence through partner collaboration is the only route.

The ability to capitalize on this potential requires firms to:

☐ Know when to collaborate.

☐ Choose which collaboration model to use.

☐ Derive the expected value from collaborative relationships.

☐ Understand the industry decisions that are made as the economy becomes increasingly networked.

Only by articulating and implementing a clear strategy in these areas, will firms be able to achieve the greatest prize, which is available from cross-business collaboration.

PART 1

DEFINING THE NEED

CHAPTER 1

CHOOSING COLLABORATIVE APPROACHES

DEFINING STRATEGY

The corporate graveyard is full of examples of organizations that chose to collaborate, when a more transactional nature of relationship would have been appropriate. Or, more commonly, firms have talked the partnership rhetoric, but continue to operate in a manner more reflective of adversarial buyer-supplier interactions.

Collaborative relationships are not easy to develop; they involve high risk, and their establishments and operation carry a high resource burden, not just in terms of quantity, but quality – collaborative relationships need the firm's best people. Thus, choosing whether or not to collaborate in a particular area of the firm's scope is critical. The decision can be made by considering the question: 'Is the business objective, which the collaborative relationship would deliver, strategic?'

AN ORGANIZATIONAL FRAMEWORK

How do we define whether something is strategic? More importantly, how do we define the scope of the area where we are considering looking for a collaborative partner or partners? The four European firms that got together to create the Eurofighter took a very different view on scope to Wal-Mart who collaborated with Procter and Gamble, and to BP when it outsourced HR management to Exult. There are four elements of a firm's operating envelope that each need to be considered when evaluating whether collaboration is an appropriate strategy; each then drives a different model of collaboration.

1 **Business processes** – Which focus on the actual work activity of the organization.

2 **Organizational capability** – Defined as the collective functional or technical competences of the corporation.

3 **Value proposition** – Focused on the unique set of benefits the organization is attempting to deliver to its target customers, which drives its product and service offering.

4 **Channel management** – Which considers the current and possible routes to market for the firm's products and services.

For each of these four dimensions, the critical starting point is to understand how the strategy of the organization deploys into each of these areas, and what scope that gives to consider the use of collaborative strategies.

DEPLOYING STRATEGY

For any evaluation of strategic importance to be effective we need to know the strategy. More specifically, we need to identify the strategy by a language and a set of terms that enables us to relate it to the four areas of process, capability, proposition and channel. Often this is where firms struggle. Kaplan and Norton, in their ground breaking research in the early 1990s that led to the creation of the balanced scorecard, found that nine out of ten organizations failed to achieve the strategic goals they set themselves. Why? Because they were unable to take often carefully thought through and well-crafted strategic aims, and convert them into meaningful guidance and resource prioritization, necessary to execute the aspiration.

Achieving that goal is a necessary precursor to be able to assess strategic fit from a collaboration perspective. Using some of the balanced scorecard principles can help us do that effectively. Fundamentally, to enable deployment, the firm's strategy needs to be converted into a set of meaningful objectives statements that define:

☐ Direction (e.g. we wish to grow market share).

☐ Focus (e.g. within the high-end financial services sector).

☐ Degree (e.g. by 2 per cent year on year for the next three years).

At its simplest level, a company needs a set of strategic objective statements, which are specific and quantified where possible and cover the full scope of the strategic aspiration of the firm. Hence, balanced scorecard thinking in terms of shareholder, customer, process and innovation and learning can assist in this process. Once the strategy is in a deployed state, we can consider how this can be evaluated along each of these four areas of potential collaboration.

BUSINESS PROCESS ASSESSMENT

Since the Industrial Revolution changed the shape of the trading world, organizations have been structured almost always around functional skills set; professional silos where expertise won over customer focus. This all began to change with the arrival of the quality revolution, pioneered by Demming, Baldridge *et al.* They spoke, for the first time, of the concept of business processes, rather than functional stove-pipes, forming the basis for understanding how work was done and how customer expectations were met.

The explosive best-seller by Hammer and Champy[1], which focused purely on the concept of business processes and how they could be re-engineered, made this vocabulary commonplace in the business world. This now provides a common basis for evaluating collaboration scope with regard to the existing operations of an organization. Hammer and Champy define a

[1] Michael Hammer and James Champy, *Reengineering the Corporation*, Harper Business, 1993.

business process as, 'a collection of activities that takes one or more kind of inputs and creates an output of value to the customer'.

To understand whether a business process is strategic to an organization, and subsequently, whether it is appropriate for collaboration, we must first develop a process model for the firm. It is important to recognize that organizations operate two distinctly different types of processes:

1 **Core processes** – Which take market opportunities and convert them into money in the bank.

2 **Support processes** – Which ensure that the core processes operate effectively.

For a typical organization, there will be no more than ten of either core or support processes that collectively encompass the entire work architecture of the firm.

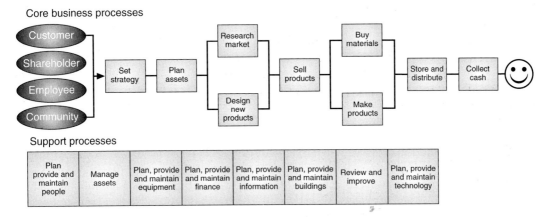

FIGURE 1.1: Example of a business process model

Strategy applied to process

Processes are defined as strategic, depending on the degree to which they achieve the stated aims of the firm. This means that over time, as the strategy moves on, different process areas may become more or less strategic. Take the provision of Information Technology (IT) – during the 1980s many financial services institutions around the globe outsourced this process, because they felt it was peripheral to their core business. As the communications revolution moved on in the 1990s, those same firms began to realize that the technology, which linked their customers to delivery mechanisms such as the internet, hand-held mobile devices and ATM networks, was critical to future success. Hence, we have witnessed a wave of firms either in-sourcing that process, or changing the shape of the relationship with the third-party provider to one of collaboration, not transaction.

However, knowing that a process has strategic importance is not the only factor in considering its worth for collaboration – we also need to understand the current level of performance in that area. For Coca-Cola, the process of creating and maintaining brand will undoubtedly sit in the 'strategically important' category. Nevertheless, if this is an area where Coca-Cola has enormous in-house strength, and its performance in this area is in the top 10 per cent, than the need to consider third-party collaboration is going to be low. It is more likely that collaboration is needed in the areas where the strategic requirement is there, but current process performance or the expected gap that will need to be closed to achieve the strategy, demand attention. This is the opportunity for collaboration.

		CUSTOMER REQUIREMENTS				
		Product/Service availability	Competitive price	Easy, efficient order and returns process	Helpful, friendly and efficient staff	Quality and reliability
PROCESSES	Research market		✗	✗	✗	✗
	Design new products		✗			
	Sell products	✗	✗	✗		✗
	Buy materials	✗	✗			✗
	Store and distribute	✗		✗	✗	
	Collect cash			✗	✗	

TABLE 1.1: Strategy applied to business process

A change in strategy is one of the most common reasons for firms to consider taking a collaboration route to process delivery. The mobile telecommunications industry is a good example. From the early 1990s until around 2000, in almost every telecommunications market, the strategic focus for firms was customer acquisition – growing subscriber numbers as the market matured to cover the high fixed costs invested in the network. During this time, the processes of creating market demand and converting sales opportunities were key. Suddenly, market penetration was achieved, the WAP revolution did not happen, and Third Generation (3G) technology was still two to three years away from commercial and operational viability. Almost overnight, customer retention and growth, rather than acquisition, became the strategic priority. Therefore, now the processes of delivering customer service, managing customer relationships and delivering product and service enhancements – in short the CRM (Customer Relationship Management) processes – have become top of the pile. However, for many telecommunications firms, these were processes that had received no investment, focus or time. Yet as of now, they had to deliver the firm's strategic objectives.

This is when the potential for collaboration arises. Vodafone, France Telecom or Airtouch do not necessarily have to operate their own customer interactivity centres; they do not have to build all the data needed to effect a CRM strategy – their hardware providers, such as Nokia or Ericsson will already have much of this. Self-service websites for customers will be of increasing importance, but provided that message and the brand are carried, the company that builds, maintains and operates the sites can be outside the firms' borders. In short, transforming these processes quickly might be achieved more effectively by finding someone who already does them well, rather than trying to start redesigning the existing in-house activities to meet the standard required. This is not just about the firm's own processes; collaborating with suppliers and customers to take a broader, end-to-end view of the activity flow from primary producer to end customers can utilize exactly the same tools and approaches.

ORGANIZATIONAL CAPABILITY EVALUATION

Processes reflect the work activity of the organization. However, simply understanding their scope and deliverables is not the only strategic enabler for an organization. Is the firm capable of operating processes? Many firms spent the 1990s re-engineering their processes, only to find that when they implemented what appeared to be best practice designs, the results were not what they expected. This was because they did not have the organizational capability to manage newly designed business processes. Or, as Gary Hamel and C K Prahlahaad might say – they had not understood their core competencies.

Capability, for the purposes of collaboration evaluation, is more than just a strength, a competence or a stand-alone technology. It describes a highly bundled and deeply embedded set of competencies, technologies and processes that house an organization's collective know-how. It is an ability to turn strategic vision into executed action by having all the necessary elements in a particular area to enable that.

Sony developed a capability for miniaturization, and utilized this in the production of the Walkman, the Camcorder, the Watchman and many other products. This capability encompassed a set of proprietary technologies, R&D and New Product Development & Introduction (NPD&I) processes, and critical skills within teams of staff. McDonald's have built their global business from a capability in product service know-how, Canon upon a foundation of optics know-how delivering market leadership in cameras, fax machines and electronic imaging.

Defining where the scope for potential collaboration could lie means answering two questions:

1 How do I define what my capabilities are?

2 How do I know if they are strategic or not?

Defining capabilities

Organizations build capabilities for one purpose, and one purpose only. To enable them to deliver their marketplace promise. Or, to be specific, to enable them to make, transport and sell their chosen products and services in a manner that will differentiate them from their competitors. That is the starting point for defining capability sets. Consider an imaginary chain of petrol filling stations as an example. To be successful this organization needs:

- [ ] A broad base of filling locations.
- [ ] A recognized brand.
- [ ] Competitively priced fuel, with perhaps some form of loyalty mechanism.
- [ ] A good range of products sold from the forecourt shop.

Behind each of these key success factors, the organization will need capabilities to deliver them. Some capabilities support just one marketplace success factor, others support multiple. Collectively they are the set of capabilities that the organization needs to be successful. These would include:

- [ ] Location planning (being able to find good locations to purchase or lease forecourt space).
- [ ] Brand management.
- [ ] Financial market management (for protecting fuel prices).
- [ ] Supply chain management (for delivering fuel to the forecourt).

☐ Category management (for choosing the right range of products and services to stock on the forecourt).

For this simple example of an organization, there are probably 30–40 capabilities that are needed to achieve a differentiated position in the marketplace.

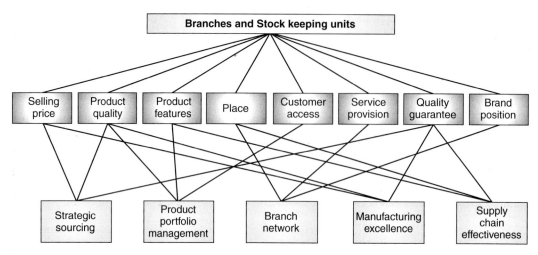

FIGURE 1.2: Framework for defining capability

Evaluating strategic capabilities

We know what our capabilities are, but which ones are truly strategic, and therefore a possible candidate for collaboration? There are six simple tests to apply to each capability to answer this question:

1 **Competitive test** – Is this potential capability better than those of our competitors?

2 **Imitation test** – Is it a capability that, if fully developed, would be difficult for our competitors to imitate?

3 **Customer test** – Does this capability make a disproportionate contribution to the perceived customer benefits?

4 **Value test** – Would we be able to either command a price premium as a result of fully developing this benefit, or a material cost advantage?

5 **Strategic test** – How much can this capability impact upon our industry position?

6 **Market test** – Can this capability provide access to and leverage in a wide variety of markets, whether geographic or segment based?

A simple deployment matrix can assist to gain clarity in this area. Once the list of core capabilities are known, the following questions can be asked in all of the four models of strategic collaboration (supply chain, capability, proposition-based and competitive) – is this something we could achieve faster, cheaper or more sustainably through a partner than by attempting to build it ourselves?

CORE COMPETENCIES / TESTS	STRATEGIC SOURCING	PRODUCT PORTFOLIO MANAGEMENT	BRANCH NETWORK	MANUFACTURING EXCELLENCE	SUPPLY CHAIN EFFECTIVENESS	RETAIL STORE MANAGED SYSTEMS	BRAND MANAGEMENT	COST CONTROL	MARKETING	FINANCIAL RESOURCES
❶ VERSUS COMPETITORS (Better/Same/Worse)										
❷ DIFFICULTY TO IMITATE (Hard/Moderate/Easy)										
❸ CONTRIBUTION TO CUSTOMER BENEFIT (Large/Medium/Small)										
❹ COMMAND A PRICE OR COST ADVANTAGE (Large/Medium/Small)										
❺ IMPORTANCE TO INDUSTRY POSITION (Major/Minor/None)										
❻ PROVIDE ACCESS AND LEVERAGE IN WIDE VARIETY OF MARKETS (High/Medium/Low)										

TABLE 1.2: Deployment matrix for core capabilities

VALUE PROPOSITION CREATION

IBM spent the 1980s focusing on its mainframe competitors, while Apple was creating the micro-computing marketplace and stealing IBM's short-term future. Later, IBM viewed Intel and Microsoft as junior partners, practically putting them into business, but failing to recognize the future threat they posed. Sears focused its anti-competitive aggression at J C Penney and Montgomery Ward, while Wal-Mart stole a march, now sitting on the number one spot in the Fortune 500. What did the winners do in this list that made a difference? They did not try and outplay their competitors; in fact, they did not try to understand what they were doing. Instead, they focused solely on the customer and developed new propositions that offered superior benefits at lower costs and formed new markets. This is how it can be with collaboration.

Many organizations, when considering strategy, see it in the same manner as a general marshalling troops. Where should resources be focused? Which battles are more important to the overall success of the war? This tends to lead to an internally focused prioritization against known service offerings and familiar marketplaces. Value propositions start from a different place: the customer.

Creating value propositions

Three MBA students have just finished their studies. They decide that rather than join the ranks of the employed, they wish to start up a new business. They sit and consider their options, reviewing all types of industry sectors, product and service ideas, including where to start the business from. Should it be in the States, a European base, or perhaps a low-cost location such as South Africa, India or Sri Lanka? Nothing is ruled out, everything is possible. The scope of their thinking is unbounded.

For organizations with current products and services, executives with existing functions or business units to protect, and investors with an aversion to risk, this type of open thinking is challenging. Yet it is necessary if value propositions are to be developed. The starting point for achieving this is to understand clearly the value equation:

$$\text{Value} = f\,(\text{Benefits-Cost})$$

Where benefits are the set of advantages that a customer gains from purchasing the product or service mix, and cost is the perceived total cost of ownership (covering price, payment terms, cost of doing business, error, re-work costs and so on). In creating value propositions, we seek to find product and service combinations that deliver greater value to a particular group of customers – a segment.

The first step is to define the total customer population that we wish to consider. This may be an existing customer base or it may be the entire potential market (consumer or business) within the geographic markets in which we operate. Any boundary is acceptable, but the lines must be drawn.

Once we know our total customer set, the challenge is to understand what our customers are attempting to deliver to their customers or the end-consumer – what their marketplace differentiators are. They will only purchase things from their suppliers or providers, which they feel help them to achieve their own strategic goals. If this takes us into a consumer marketplace, then it is a case of understanding how purchasing behaviour supports consumers' lifestyle priorities. When we are clear on these customer or consumer priorities, we can begin to understand how the product or service arena that our own firm operates in contributes to these goals, not in terms of product characteristics, but by defining the benefits that the customers require. The benefits can then determine the product characteristics, but we need to start with the desired outcome first, which is the final proposition sold to the end-consumer.

Retail banking provides an example. For a particular customer group, perhaps busy professionals, simplicity and 24-hour access may be the desired benefits they want from their provider. Understanding these benefits allows a complete tailoring of the product and service mix to this segment – from simplified forms, a single password for all accounts, free WAP or internet banking provision, right through to new marketplace concepts like a single account for mortgage, savings, current account and credit cards. When Virgin launched this new concept in the UK market, leading with a brand new value proposition, it did so by creating collaborative relationships with the likes of Royal Bank of Scotland to make it happen and not by being able to build all the necessary infrastructure to deliver it. Virgin developed the value proposition, which required more than Virgin's in-house scope of activities to deliver it, and therefore the company collaborated to make it happen.

In summary, what Virgin did for retail banking, many others have done in different industries. Direct Line Insurance went from zero to 30 per cent market share in a year, by breaking the model of service provision in insurance; South West Airlines created an airline operated like a bus service; and Monsanto created end-market brands like Lycra from the starting point of first place value chain position in the chemicals industry. Focus on customer benefits, develop a product and service mix (a value proposition), which delivers a greater set of those benefits, and then consider the delivery mechanism to achieve that. And again, if that delivery mechanism requires capabilities, processes, technologies, customer bases, scale, investment or management that you do not have, collaboration could be the answer.

CHANNEL MANAGEMENT

A company may operate the best business processes, with the relevant capabilities, offering the greatest marketplace proposition, yet if someone else controls the route to market, it could all be in vain. Did Microsoft invent the best operating platform? Does Novartis make the best seeds? Do GlaxoSmithKline (gsk) always develop the best drugs? Is Coca-Cola really the best tasting drink on the planet? The market researchers can answer the yes or no to these questions; the important thing that links each of these four examples together is the organizations' focus on dominating the route to the customer: the channel.

For the past decade, channel management has become an increasingly strategic issue. Not just within organizations, but also for politicians, competition commissioners and lawyers. Microsoft's case of channel dominance is well documented and publicised. However, there are many more cases across most sectors. As industries consolidate, being able to manipulate traditional 'true' markets where supply and demand equations lead to price positions in favour of the supply providers, is a proven route to 'super profits'. The UK supermarkets grew their total share from below 30 per cent to above 50 per cent of food provision in a ten-year period. Suddenly, five major players could hold even giants like Heinz and Kelloggs to ransom.

Identifying new channel strategies

The starting point to identify new channel opportunities is the same as developing value propositions. Define the target customer population. For channel strategy, the simple next question is, 'Who currently controls those customers?' In the UK, Centrica, the power utility, bought the AA, a car breakdown and recovery service, but not to diversify its industry position. It did it to access the AA's millions of customers. Airlines, hotels and car hire companies collaborate routinely. The target customer of one is held 'captive' by the other, at the point of their next purchasing decision. Furthermore, the opportunity is much broader than this.

Channel collaboration touches the heart of economic and competitive theory. It attempts to break the business assumption that customer loyalty and customer satisfaction are connected in a linear way. When Thomas Jones and W Earl Sasser Jr analyzed the trends between these two data points, taking repurchase as the acid test of loyalty, they found a wide variation across industries. For customers who scored satisfaction of two out of five, their repurchase levels were roughly:

- ☐ 100 per cent for their local telephone operator.
- ☐ 70 per cent for their regional airline provider.
- ☐ 40 per cent for their local hospital.
- ☐ 20 per cent for their PC provider.
- ☐ Less than 5 per cent for their automotive supplier.

Why did two out of five not deliver the same result all round? Simply because the supply and demand landscape in each industry was different. For the local telephone operator, most respondents came from areas where there was either a monopolistic or quasi-monopolistic arrangement. At the other end of the scale, the automotive industry has huge over-supply, a mass of existing and new competitors and enormous customer choice, in terms of both models and in methods of buying.

Therefore, identifying potential collaborative channel partners is not about an internal assessment, aside from defining the target population. It is instead an analysis of which organizations have relationships with your target customer base, and what potential exists for using that market power to transfer supply-demand imbalance to your product and service offering.

MARKET ASSESSMENT

We have studied our strategic goals, and considered whether a process, capability, value proposition or channel gap exists. Now for the second critical question: 'Are there external parties with greater resources, capabilities or market power that could enable the business goal to be delivered more easily?' Recognizing a need is one thing, finding somebody who can fulfill it is something different altogether.

Clearly delineating between the needs of process, capability, value proposition and channel is a helpful starting point. Many firms, when they look for partners, have a clouded view of what they are looking for. They may try to discuss a broad range of opportunities with potential partners, not truly understanding the specific need they are trying to meet. Even where the market assessment identifies the same potential organization for more than one of the need areas, the debate should be engaged separately for each. The shared goals, commercial model and *modus operandi* for a capability collaboration are so different from a value proposition collaboration, that trying to manage them as a single entity will only bring confusion.

The great benefit of a clear internal assessment, using frameworks for each of the four need areas, is that these precise same frameworks are the structure for conducting the market assessment. However, what all four will have in common is that to enable a market search to take place, the requirements for the collaboration, whether they be process expertise or channel control, need to be translated into a set of demographic requirements. Typically these will include:

- ☐ Industry and sector focus.
- ☐ Customer base and structure of relationship.
- ☐ Market sectors.
- ☐ Channel split.
- ☐ Risk profile.
- ☐ New product/service pipeline.
- ☐ Legal actions.
- ☐ Geographic location.
- ☐ Financial standing and performance.
- ☐ Product and service offering.
- ☐ Existing collaborative relationships.
- ☐ Patents/technology ownership.

The outcome of such a market assessment will be a list of potential collaborative partners based on the 'hard facts'. From here, an understanding develops about whether theoretical strategic fit can lead into shared delivery of greater profits, customer value creation and long-term competitive advantage.

MODELS OF COLLABORATION

Business strategy can be applied to fours areas – process, capability, value proposition and channel – where collaborative relationships can enable the firm's aspirations to be met in a faster, cheaper or more able way. For each of these four areas, a unique type of collaborative model can develop:

- ☐ For business process gaps, a supply chain collaboration will provide the solution.
- ☐ Missing core capabilities demand a capability-based collaboration.
- ☐ Where new value propositions have been developed, a proposition-based collaboration is required.
- ☐ For organizations attempting to control the channel to market, a competitive collaboration will result.

Understanding the strategic need and identifying the right collaborative model is the starting point. A specific set of tools, approaches and frameworks for the chosen model is the next step to make the collaboration promise come alive. For each of the models, there are six areas to consider:

1 What are the *goals and scope* of the collaboration?

2 What are the *key drivers*?

3 Which *commercial structure* is most appropriate, and what ownership issues can that drive?

4 What are the most appropriate planning *tools* to use in evaluating the collaboration?

5 What sort of *operating model* is necessary?

6 What are the *common pitfalls* and how can they be avoided?

SUMMARY

1 Collaborative relationships involve high risk, resource commitment and a long-term view. As a result, they should only be used for a firm's strategic priorities.

2 In order to understand whether an area is strategic, the business strategy needs to identify first clear objectives and measures.

3 Four areas can be considered to identify where strategic collaboration could play a role:

☐ Business processes.

☐ Organizational capability.

☐ Value proposition development and delivery.

☐ Channel management.

4 The opportunity for collaboration can be assessed by deploying the business strategy into each of these four areas.

5 Understanding a strategic need must then be matched with a mechanism for identifying potential collaborative parties.

6 Once the need for collaboration has been identified, the tools used to identify need can be used to assess the market for potential partners.

7 For each area of collaboration, a different collaboration model should be applied, namely supply chain, capability, proposition-based or competitive.

PART 2

FOUR MODELS OF COLLABORATION

CHAPTER 2

SUPPLY CHAIN COLLABORATION

GOALS AND SCOPE

The supply chain of an organization is the sum of the core business process as from customer requirements to cash in the bank. Supply chain collaborations have business process at their heart. The business process may be part of the internal processes that a firm has chosen to deliver through a partner, or at the interface with either suppliers or customers, where the organization's process extends further up or down the industry value chain. This makes the issue of scope an easy one for supply chain collaborations.

For example, let's examine an organization, which chooses to use a collaborative partner to deliver one of its own business processes. That process can be defined by agreeing a series of parameters:

☐ **Purpose** – What is the process there to do?

☐ **Scope** – Where does the process start and end?

☐ **Inputs** – What are the initiators of the process?

☐ **Key activities** – What are the high level steps of the process?

☐ **Outputs** – What does the process deliver or produce?

If, for instance, the internal process considered for delivery by a collaborative partner was to prepare quotations against customer enquiries, the scope definition could be the following:

☐ **Process** – Prepare quotation.

☐ **Purpose** – Win the right business.

☐ **Scope** – From receipt of enquiry to follow up of result.

☐ **Inputs** – Enquiry: written, verbal, electronic data exchange (EDI), external influences (e.g. exchange rates, raw material prices).

29

☐ **Key activities**

1 Review enquiry.

2 Prepare/update draft design (if not existing).

3 Sample request.

4 Determine cost.

5 Agree selling price and delivery availability.

6 Prepare written quotation and data sheet.

7 Submit quote to customer.

8 Follow up opportunity.

9 Accept order or close-down quote.

10 Understand reason for win/loss.

☐ **Outputs** – Quotation, no-quote decision, summary of results, review.

What this simple template provides is clarity of interface between the collaborative partners. Standards can be developed around the input and output deliverables. The activities which need to be delivered to convert inputs into outputs can easily be monitored and reviewed.

For internal processes, not only is the scope relatively easy to define, provided there is a clearly understood process model where each process has a descriptive template, but so are the goals. Processes are managed through the use of process measurements, and the precise same philosophy can be applied to goals. Given that we know what the output expectation is from the process, we need to be able to monitor three elements that make up the goals of that process:

1 **Cost** – What is the unit cost of the output deliverables?

2 **Pace** – How quickly can the process steps be executed, converting the input into the output?

3 **Excellence** – What quality and service standards do the final outputs achieve?

Reconsider the 'Prepare quotation' process. The goals of that process, and therefore the goals of a collaboration to deliver this process, could be:

☐ **Cost** – Cost per quote produced, investment cost of lost quotes.

☐ **Pace** – Elapsed time from quote request to quote delivered or no quote decision communicated; elapsed time from quote delivered to client yes/no decision.

☐ **Excellence** – Conversion rate of quote to business.

Therefore, for the instance where the review of business process identified that a supply chain collaboration could deliver that strategic objective better, the focus and goals are defined by making the process scope and measurement the basic tools around which to build consensus with the collaboration partner. What happens, however, when the collaboration extends outside the firms' own scope of activities and into the industry value chain?

Supplier and customer supply chain collaboration

When Wal-Mart began its process of engaging the supplier community to play a greater role in delivering its marketplace promise, it recognized that its strategic suppliers, like Procter and

Gamble, were better able to manage fulfillment onto the supermarket shelf than Wal-Mart were. This is precisely what Wal-Mart asked Procter and Gamble to do.

As previously discussed, within organizations almost half of all error and re-work occurs at the departmental boundaries. When that same analysis is applied to an industry value chain, the numbers are the same, if not greater. Most corporations have run cross-functional re-engineering projects, attempting to get sales, marketing, procurement and manufacturing to work together to achieve a common design and to deliver greater overall value. For most, this has been challenging. Individuals approach problem solving from their functional position and evaluate solutions based on diverging strategic objectives. Imagine applying this to cross-company interfaces.

The methodology for achieving cross-company process is the same as for an internal company process. Forget for a moment that the process steps cut across an organizational boundary. Bring together the individuals from the respective organizations that control all the steps of the process and define them. Define the purpose, scope, inputs, activities and outputs of the total process. Agree the cost, pace and excellence targets that the process should deliver. The scope and goals of the collaboration clearly are now laid out. The challenge is how to deliver that improvement potential when the organization boundaries may work against that desired operating model.

Will the process be operated with common and shared information? Is the organization which is closest to the end-customer prepared to give its suppliers visibility of sales orders at the same moment that it acquires that knowledge? Will the checking loops that happen at both sides of an organizational interface be stopped? If it is sensible for some of the activities to be conducted by a different organization than the current one, is that acceptable?

For supply chain collaboration, clarity on scope and goals can be achieved by leveraging the process methodology; the great challenge for those that extend the scope of the value chain is to turn clarity on paper into benefits in operational performance.

KEY DRIVERS

In order that the success of the collaboration can be monitored, it is important to be clear about the business drivers. There are critical descriptors specific and unique to the key drivers of this model of collaboration.

Scope of activity

A supply chain collaboration involves no increase in the total scope of activities being performed. If collaborating to deliver an internal process, the organization's scope of activities are entirely unchanged, it is rather a case of who is executing the activity. For supply chain collaborations where the focus is on extending shared delivery up and down the industry value chain, ownership for particular tasks may swap between organizations, but they are the same tasks that were performed before the collaboration existed.

Indeed, where supply chain collaborations do begin to extend the scope of activities, they run the risk of failure because they are entering a new collaboration model for which the structure, tools and approaches for supply chain collaboration have not been designed.

Focus of collaboration

Given that the scope of activity is unchanged, the focus of the collaboration can be in two areas only. The focus may be to be cheaper (lower unit cost per delivered output) or to be better (higher service standards as defined by customers). These success factor can be monitored quite easily through the performance goals of cost (cheaper), pace and excellence (better). Again, it is not about offering more, or creating new routes to the marketplace; a supply chain collaboration model exists to simply deliver the firm's existing products and services in a way that is either more efficient or more effective than the organization could achieve by using its own resources.

Typical number of parties

While there can be no hard and fast rules for internal processes, which have moved into a supply chain collaboration model, normally this would be with a single partner. The enormous benefit (and single greatest success factor) about this model of collaboration is clarity of roles and responsibilities. Processes can be easily defined, and so can the points of interface. Orange, Mars or Coca-Cola would struggle to manage a collaboration with three parties if they chose to adopt this model to do brand management. As would AT&T, Centrica or United Utilities if they chose to collaborate for their 'bill customers' process. The most common variation to this rule of thumb is for international corporations who can easily bound geographic scopes to collaboration relationships, perhaps using different partners in Europe, the Far East and North America.

For supply chain collaboration that extends either forwards or backwards along the value chain, the edges become a little more blurred. Typically on the customer side, the one-to-one model of collaboration remains. If a major supplier to food retailers is providing product to Wal-Mart and K-Mart in a three-way collaboration, it is hard to imagine how this would be of benefit to the supplier, or an acceptable proposition to either customer. However, on the supplier side the logic is greater. Consider Conoco or Shell operating offshore oil platforms. The value chain activities being performed by all parties on that platform are for a common purpose – to optimize whole asset efficiency – and therefore bringing together what is typically five to six organizations in a single collaborative entity is the logical model.

Risk of failure

While a risk assessment will be unique to each individual collaborative relationship, regardless of model, in general supply chain collaboration carries the opportunity for the lowest risk level of all four collaboration models. If the process is managed effectively, each step towards greater collaboration can carry with it a 'regression' plan. In other words, because these are activities that the firm is currently undertaking or planning to undertake, there can always be a Plan B. Thus, for supply chain collaboration, the worry is about missing upside potential, rather than about downside damage. Although clearly the more grand the aspiration and the greater the investment (such as shared facilities or production plants), the greater this downside risk could be.

Importance of cultural fit

Quite simply, a supply chain collaboration, of whatever form, is creating an 'extended organization'. A shared sense of belonging and ownership has to be created for a set of goals, amongst a group of people from different organizational homes. For those goals to be achieved, the challenge of operating through similar values, applying common approaches to performance management, aligning incentive models and gaining broad agreement to issues of risk, decision making and focus are critical. In summary, the level of cultural fit within a supply chain collaboration needs to be at the same level deemed necessary between two functions in the same company.

COMMERCIAL STRUCTURE

Governance is an important factor in any collaborative arrangement. The softer agenda of working together, being open and building trust needs to have the hard elements of contracts, legal ownership and intellectual property rights (IPR) underpinning it.

For supply chain collaboration, the ownership of physical things is often more important than the governance of the collaboration itself. Focusing firstly on the simpler situation of internal process collaboration, the critical issues tend to concern ownership of assets, ownership of data and ownership of any IPR that is either used within the delivery of the process or evolves through improvements within business process. The simple guide for each of these areas is to ensure that accountability and authority are aligned.

Take, for example, a first tier supplier that provides car components to BMW or General Motors. If the collaboration has been set up so that the supplier is accountable for ensuring that the components are ready and available in the stock holding units on the production line, they need to have authority to manage (and therefore own) the stock up until that point, own the data relating to fill rate, reject rate and actually generate orders back into their own organization. The ownership issue clearly provides the guidance necessary to create the contractual framework. For the process to work most effectively, the supplier may need to generate purchase orders for itself, and the legal contract between the organization needs to set the rules, authority levels and mechanisms to allow that to happen within a level of risk and control acceptable to both parties. If the supplier owning stock up to the point of production makes most operational sense (i.e. the way the stock is managed), the ability to configure the stock holding units must also belong to them. The accountability to manage on-site stock must carry with it the authority to configure them to the most efficient model. Again, this therefore either requires a transfer of the physical stock holding assets to the supplier, or a 'lease' mechanism that gives the supplier *carte blanche* to change, invest or remove them as they see fit in meeting their deliverables. Ownership of the items that deliver the service, frame the key elements that the commercial contracts need to contain.

The allocation of blame

Commercial contracts tend to be rarely used if things go well, but instead are more often the mechanism by which downside risk is managed. In particular, this applies to the management of output performance standards. What happens if the error levels or reject levels are higher than expected? How is lateness evaluated? Where are cost overrun issues managed?

For supply chain collaboration, the commercial structure and service level standards are much easier to manage and monitor than in any of the other collaboration models. This is because processes have clear boundaries and easily identifiable performance targets. The same principle that applies to defining who should own assets also provides guidance in this regard. Specifically, whoever has the greatest ability to control the outcome (because they own the activities, the assets or the inputs) bears the disproportionate pain if the agreed outcome is not achieved. However, what about when activities extend up and down the industry value chain?

Extended organization commercial approaches

For this subset of supply chain collaboration, the commercial contract typically drives the ownership issues, rather than ownership informing the contract. Collaborations which cross organizational boundaries enter into a broader set of legal issues relating to competition rules and fair procurement practice. The critical considerations tend to revolve around two key areas:

1 Where does the value chain transaction actually take place (i.e. when does the supplier transfer ownership of the product or service to the customer at each step)?

2 How much sharing of information across the parties involved is allowable, so that competitive equality is not compromised?

Once these issues of transfer of ownership and permissible levels of data exchange are agreed, the more specific considerations of who works where, what they do and who owns the 'nuts and bolts' assets of delivery can be assessed.

Governance options

When it is clear who is accountable, who has authority for delivery within the collaboration, and also where legal ownership of people, assets and information sit, the final element is to design an appropriate governance model that supports effective operation. For supply chain collaboration this can be considered along two vectors:

1 Does the management of strategic versus operational issues need to be split, or can it be managed by the same group?

2 Is leadership within the collaboration driven by a single entity, or shared?

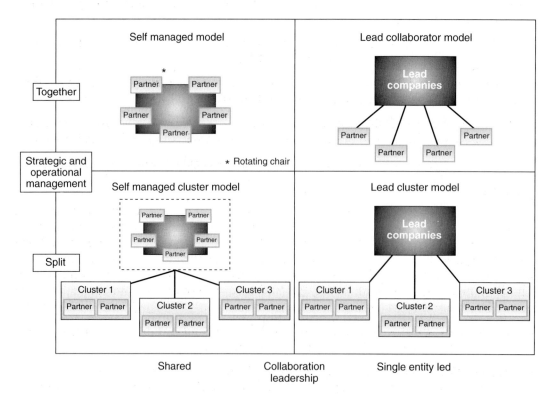

FIGURE 2.1: Governance options

Let us return to the example of the offshore oil platform which is collectively delivered by a collaborative venture of five to six organizations. Typically for a large-scale complex collaboration, the need to address strategic issues, such as the overall risk and reward model, major investment choices and key trade-offs, should be managed by a different group to that managing daily operations (e.g. today's topside efficiency or maintenance person-hour productivity record). Contrast that with a one-to-one relationship between a supplier and customer who are, for instance, jointly managing order fill rate from a production facility into a final assembly line. Here, the core team managing that operation is probably best placed to conduct the quarterly or six-monthly review of ongoing strategic direction.

For most supply chain collaborations, the simple answer to what is the appropriate governance model moving forward, is to imitate the structure that was necessary to design the collaboration in the first place. If a single group of multi-company employees could design and establish the collaboration, then on an ongoing basis, strategic and operational issues should be dealt with associatively. If it took the drive and focus of one of the organizations to make the collaboration happen, it is likely that continued success will require that role to be played again.

PLANNING TOOLS

Developing the goals, scope and structure for a supply chain collaboration can be greatly assisted by a set of appropriate and proven tools. For this collaboration model, the most commonly used techniques are:

☐ **Process analysis** – In order to create a single and common view of the work architecture, which forms the basis of the collaboration.

☐ **Cycle time analysis** – To provide clarity of both activity time and elapsed time from the inputs to the collaboration, to its agreed deliverables.

☐ **Activity value analysis** – Focusing on how each resource element and process step contributes, or otherwise, to the agreed outputs (i.e. added value) of the collaboration.

Each of these three key tools can bring clarity, focus and enable common understanding.

Process analysis

This collaboration model is based around a business process, or set of business processes and so a common and agreed map, which describes the activities that the collaboration partners jointly execute, is critical. We have already seen how a process descriptor template can bring clarity to goals and scope; and so it is with a process map for both operational management and improvement potential. The core process map needs, as its basis, to have an agreed set of symbols around which the work activity can be described. Best practice process maps tend to have symbols for six key areas:

1 **Input/output** – Identifies either the trigger for the process starting (e.g. an order, a request, a forecast) or the deliverable that completes the process.

2 **Activity** – Defines each step within the process. This can be at varying levels from the top-level process as a whole, right down to tasks that comprise each activity. The activity box needs to identify the owner of that activity step, and also who the customer and supplier of the activity are.

3 **Decision** – Identifies where the process activity could go down more than one possible path, depending on a particular criteria or management decision.

4 **Document** – Highlights where either a physical document is used or produced (such as an order form, a purchase order, a management report).

5 **IT interface** – Shows each point along the process where either data is entered into an IT system, or where information is drawn from a system to enable that step to happen.

6 **Review point** – Highlights where there is a formal review activity, potentially between collaboration partners, along the process journey. Again this box needs to define the owner and participants for that review.

With this level of clarity, the process can then be reviewed for issue areas (such as 'red flagging'), and for opportunities to remove process steps. In general, the process map provides the framework for almost all other tools, such as cycle time and activity value analysis.

Cycle time analysis

Speed is of increasing importance in many process areas, and has often been the prime driver for supply chain collaboration. The process map can form the backdrop for understanding performance in this area. For each activity step there are two things that drive process cycle time:

1 The actual time it takes to conduct the activity step.

2 The elapsed time on either side, which may be due to decision making, system waiting time, batch processing or a host of other reasons. With clarity of the total cycle time, opportunity for improvement can be targeted through a root cause evaluation. For activity time the process itself may need to be redesigned – whereas elapsed time may require new policies, information provision or authority levels.

Cycle time analysis is a powerful tool that can directly link into the collaboration goal for standards of speed. If the agreed standard is not being met, then the split of activity and elapsed time for each process step highlights where an opportunity to close the gap may come from.

Activity value analysis

Do the activities that take place add value? More specifically, do the individuals that work in the process, from whichever collaborative partner, spend their days doing added value activities? Often, individuals spend their time doing many other things in addition to the activities highlighted by the process map – holding meetings, conducting reviews, expediting orders, solving staff issues and so on.

Put simply, an activity is defined as adding value if it contributes to delivering the agreed outputs of the process, and therefore of the collaboration. Anything else, by definition, is non-added value. Here, it is most helpful if the starting point for analysis is not the process steps, but the daily schedule of staff. What does a Day In The Life Of (DILO) for staff members look like? What percentage of their time is spent doing those activities in the process map that deliver the end goal, versus other reactive or error tasks that often actually consume the day? DILO studies are a great tool for identifying added value activity, and essentially involve either staff keeping diaries, or direct observation by a third party.

In summary, once we have understood what the process map is, what cycle time performance is and what activity value is taking place, we can clearly link the collaboration goals of cost, pace and excellence (CPE), back to the actual manner in which resource is consumed and activities executed.

OPERATING MODEL

We have discussed governance and commercial structures, but on a day-to-day basis, how does the collaboration actually operate? We can answer this by considering five elements.

Physical location

Where should staff from the collaborating firms sit? Should they stay within the boundaries of their home company offices, co-locate together or all move to one of the partner's facilities? For supply chain collaboration this question is easier to answer than for other models. The process map defines what activities take place within the collaboration, and who carries out each of the steps. Where individuals should locate becomes a simple question of cost and effectiveness. In other words, take the output measurements of cost, pace and excellence, and examine how different location models impact the performance on each of the vectors. If investment is required, than a Return On Investment (ROI) equation can be used. Does the improvement in CPE justify the expenditure, based on the agreed time-scale for required return?

Location may also be affected by the outcome to the ownership question. If Procter and Gamble own stock on a supermarket chain's shelves, then that chain might be a good place for the appropriate staff to be located. If you are collectively running an offshore oil platform, or even an onshore chemical plant, the answer is you co-locate.

Points of interface

How should employees of the respective collaborative organizations interface? Is it a formal or informal model; does it happen by design or by need? Excepting the formal governance model, which may involve one or more specific structures (each carrying a pre-agreed terms of reference), operational need drives the agenda. At its simplest level, supply chain collaboration operates according to true 'extended organization' philosophies. Staff working within the collaborative entity need to behave towards one another, and therefore interface, in the same way in which employees would treat one another within their one firm.

Where collaborations have co-located the interface question becomes irrelevant – you are all in the same office. Where this is not the case, it is typical to observe day-to-day interface meetings, phone calls and e-mails between the parties, particularly for those working at the operational 'sharp-end'.

Place of belonging and development

Clearly staff belong first and foremost to their employing organization. However, for most staff a company is too large an entity to be a real place of belonging. Often, within firms, it tends to be the local office, department or function where employees most feel an affiliation. This is the same with supply chain collaboration. In most instances, it is the collaborative entity, whatever form that takes, where employees find they feel a sense of ownership towards. Where firms often 'brand' the collaborative venture, this sense can be felt more strongly. This triggers a set of interesting questions: Where does responsibility for career progression, performance feedback and skills development sit? Is it with the parent organizations, or within the management structure of the collaborative entity?

The answers will vary, but in supply chain collaboration more than in any other model, experience has shown that over time staff move their centre of gravity to the collaborative entity. Examining human resource management activities upfront as an integral part of the collaboration operating model is often a necessary pre-requisite.

Role of technology

The 1990s saw the creation and explosive growth of the Enterprize Resource Planning (ERP) market. From humble beginnings, this market now generates $20 billion per year in revenues for the software vendors alone, and the market leader, SAP, has 39,000 installations and rising. The logic of the ERP revolution was to get all staff working from the same set of common and shared information; integrate transaction steps together and both operational efficiency and management decision making will be improved. Broadly the same logic applies to collaboration.

Collaborative partners will, at the starting point, each having different operating systems. Even when they have the same software badge on the front, variable configuration, different releases and unique data structures will make that apparent similarity an irrelevancy. So where now? For supply chain collaboration, the most important technology link to make is that of shared information, which feeds integrated planning. Know where customer demand or just simply inputs, are likely to come from and when. Joint decision making is greatly enabled by common information. With the arrival of Portal technology (in other words, the specific technology which is a presentation interface with the appearance of a web-front end), the ability to acquire information from a variety of source systems makes this a real and rapid reality.

More than with any other collaborative model, moving the whole collaboration onto a common transactional system will have huge benefits in precisely the same way that it would within the boundaries of an organization. Supply chain collaboration is about delivering processes at the most efficient level possible, and integrated and common technology plays a major role in achieving that goal.

Method of incentives

Responsibilities, clarity of activity steps and sharing common information are all helpful to achieve an effective supply chain collaboration. However, what about money? The acid test of alignment is often most clearly communicated by the method staff are paid and the way bonuses are decided. For supply chain collaboration, the extended organization principle applies: clear scope and goals, operating as a single entity. Therefore, wherever possible, the *modus operandi* should add a common pay model to the other elements of the human resource management agenda.

Often, the pragmatic reality of aligning pay and bonus models is too much. Organizations from a fragmented pay scheme history, often find policy alignment too challenging within their own corporate boundaries, let alone across them. However, the creation of a common bonus pool, or even a 'kicker' bonus (i.e. a non-contractual bonus that rewards high achievement), is something that can often be brought into play when trying to ensure that staff from all companies are marching to the same beat.

COMMON PITFALLS

In the same way that each of the four collaboration models has its own unique goals, drivers and operating model, they each carry their own set of familiar pitfalls. For supply chain collaboration the critical ones are:

☐ **Scope creep** – Supply chain collaboration's greatest asset is an absolute clarity of scope and deliverables. This can commonly lead to more than supply chain collaboration. Resist this, at least in the first few years of the collaboration's existence, otherwise this critical benefit area can be lost.

☐ **Focus on fit** – Supply chain relationships operate from the extended organization concept. As such, it is commonplace to find staff from multiple organizations working side by side, in the same location, trying to achieve the same goal, but employed by different parent companies. For this to be an effective 'on the ground' model, cultural fit plays a significant part.

☐ **Use the tools** – Because processes can be readily analyzed through a set of proven approaches, a clear foundation for success exists. Make sure that the facts allow the collaboration to develop clear and robust plans which fully utilize these available approaches.

☐ **Be target driven** – Cost, pace and excellence. Almost regardless of industry, process area or geographic boundary, the goals of a supply chain collaboration can be distilled into clear goals for these three areas. Allow that to lead the debate.

☐ **Enable regression** – Risk can be firmly managed in the supply chain model. The scope of activities does not increase through the supply chain's creation, and therefore all activities have a current procedure. This allows for easy regression should the worst happen; ensuring that a backward path is always available is a critical success factor for the collaborations evolution.

☐ **Aim high** – Supply chain collaborations most frequently occur between existing customer–supplier relationships. Whilst this brings benefits of fit, it also came at constraint of incremental thinking. Challenge this constantly; focusing instead on innovative solutions.

SUMMARY

1 Supply chain collaboration uses the principles of business process management at the core of its approach.

2 Using a template approach to defining business process can allow for simple clarity on the scope and goals of the collaboration.

3 Supply chain collaboration goals can be grouped under the three areas of cost, pace and excellence.

4 Supply chain collaboration splits into two broad categories – one that involves a partner delivering an internal process to an organization, and one that extends up or down the industry value chain to suppliers or customers.

5 Where the collaboration relates to internal processes, ownership of data, assets and IPR should drive the commercial model; where it is a collaboration that extends up or down the industry value chain, the commercial model should drive ownership issues.

6 The three most useful tools for planning collaboration potentials are process mapping, cycle time analysis and activity value analysis.

7   The *modus operandi* of a supply chain collaboration is principally based around the philosophy of the extended organization – treating all those working within the collaboration as if they worked for the same entity, operating from common processes, HR practices, technology systems, locations and pay and reward models.

CHAPTER 3

CAPABILITY-BASED COLLABORATION

GOALS AND SCOPE

Processes, which form the basis for supply chain collaboration are clear, definable and concrete. Capabilities are, regrettably, less easy to articulate. Where does the capability for 'brand management' begin and end; and what exactly does it contain? Or for 'logistics and network management'? Does that include demographic profiling as well as truck maintenance? What is the scope for such a capability area?

And the difficulty does not stop there. What about the goals? Processes have clear goals; outputs you can touch. What about capabilities? What target is applied to McDonald's capability for service? On its own, the capability does not achieve anything. Being great at research and development (R&D) does not help a pharmaceutical firm. Creating blockbuster drugs is good – having the best scientific minds an interesting by-product, but nothing to excite the company's shareholders unless this is turned into marketable products that create revenue. So how do you set goals and define the scope of a capability-based collaboration?

One plus one

Capability-based collaborations begin to move closer to more traditional alliance-based models used in the oil and gas, automative and aerospace industries in the mid 1990s. The models tried to build solid supplier relationships in order to use them as a strong source of innovation. The boundaries between each party are insufficiently clear and do not allow management of the collaboration around easily identifiable individual roles and responsibilities. Shared goals are needed. It is only when the capability of the organizations in the collaboration is delivered through the processes of the 'host' firm that marketplace objectives can be achieved. For this to be effective, the collaboration needs to deliver more than the sum of its component parts.

Many organizations, particularly smaller ones, look for an external partner to support them on legal capabilities, for example. Rather than recruit internally for all of the various skills sets required to provide legal services, the organization partners with an external firm who specializes in this area. On their own, legal skills achieve nothing in terms of organizational goals. The starting point to understand value is to consider application. Legal services may be used to support an acquisition process – the test of its success measured by achieving the acquisition and by the enhanced EPS (earnings per share) which result. Legal services may be used to support the firm during an HR issue, such as a tribunal, where the sign of success is winning the tribunal or minimizing liability payments. Alternatively, the role could be to provide ongoing HR legal advice for drafting correct employment contracts, and for ensuring that new HR legislation is enacted quickly within the organization. The measure of success this time is that no future costs are incurred due to not having covered all the bases for HR legal and contractual compliance.

To begin to put together the goals of a capability-based collaboration, we need to recognize two key things:

1 The goals will reflect the application of the capability, not the capability itself.

2 In almost all situations, therefore, application will require the input of the collaboration with other parts of the receiving organization, making goals truly shared.

Before deciding on the goals of the collaboration, there is one other critical consideration. Does the collaboration exist to provide a continuous service, or has it been set up for a one-off endeavour?

Consider the example of R&D collaboration in the life sciences sector, which is typified by the major firms using small, innovative development houses. These relationships can work in two entirely different ways that lead to quite separate types of collaboration goals:

1 Has the relationship with the development house been created to focus on the development of a specific drug?

2 Does the relationship with the development house exist as an extension of the client's R&D house to provide ongoing input?

If it is the former situation or generally for any collaboration that is project-based, then normal project goal setting approaches can be used. Often, project balanced scorecards are a helpful model. In this example, they may include financial (ROI, cost/budget), customer (patient benefit rate), process (Food and Drugs Administration approval time, test success rate) and people (knowledge development) measures.

If it is the latter relationship, the collaboration's measures of success will be the same as those of the R&D department. The collaboration will be tasked to achieve an enhancement of the targets – but not to change the fundamental targets. This is where capability-based and supply chain collaborations have an area in common – neither extend the overall scope of operations for the organization.

Collaboration scope

Given that activities of the capability-based collaboration are less bounded than in the supply chain model, scope needs to be defined more by goal parameters. The goal of the R&D collaboration is to develop a new drug between two parties – a major life sciences firm and a small development house. Pinning down what is needed to achieve this goal is difficult. Initially, work by the development house may provide the answer quickly; trials may go well and FDA approval comes speedily. Alternatively, initial research may prove to be unfruitful and additional research may need to be brought in. Facilities for that research may need to be built if existing technology is not sufficient. Even if the process gets close to the end, resistance from the FDA may require lobbying which could involve expenditure on another third party, or more reliance on the life sciences firm's own resources than originally expected. In short – we cannot scope the activities of the collaboration, although we know exactly what we are trying to achieve. So how does scope work in these kinds of collaborations?

Often the best approach is to consider scope management as a process, not as a one-time definition. The parameters are set upfront, an initial scope agreed, and then at each of the formal collaboration governance meetings, this is reviewed against the emerging requirements needed to achieve the collaboration's stated goals. The vectors to monitor scope will typically be:

☐ **Activities** – What activities can be performed within the collaboration so that the goals can be achieved, without conflicting with activities performed by any of the collaboration parties' 'home' organizations?

☐ **Cost** – What are the expenditure boundaries within which the collaboration may operate, and what are the mechanisms by which those funds are calculated and collected from the partners involved?

☐ **Resources** – How many, of what kind of resources (e.g. people, equipment, facilities) will be provided by each party, and to what level (e.g. skills, technical specification, operating standard)?

By monitoring these scope items (inputs) against goal achievement (outputs), an effective foundation can be set to manage a capability-based collaboration.

KEY DRIVERS

To monitor the success of the collaboration we need to understand the business drivers, which can be summarized as scope, focus, partners, risks and fit.

Scope of activity

Similar to supply chain collaboration, capability-based collaborations do not increase the scope of the organization's activity. Or at least, not when one considers it from an activity point of view. In most instances, capability-based collaborations are formed to enable a firm to improve what they already do, by having a greater capability to do it. The scope is not greater from a 'process' perspective, but it is often from an 'output' perspective. Our R&D collaboration is not trying to do something different to what the life sciences firm has been doing for years – there is no change to scope – but it is hoping to deliver new blockbuster drugs that it is unable to do on its own. Therefore, no change in scope of activity – rather an aspiration to get 'more bang for the buck' in terms of goal achievement.

Focus of collaboration

Given that this is a collaboration model based around skills and competencies of both a human and physical nature, the focus tends to be one of 'enhancement'. Usually it concerns achieving something that the originating organization could not achieve on its own. While this may lead ultimately to lower cost or higher customer service standards, these are not the primary focuses. An engineering department may choose to collaborate with a design house that has the latest drawing technologies that it does not have itself. The department is getting access to a capability set that allows it to produce superior outputs. This would be the same for a collaboration with a brand agency, legal services or with our R&D house.

Typical number of parties

There cannot be hard and fast rules, however, in general capability-based collaborations exist between two parties. Because of the less definable nature, and the fact that the goals will either be project-based, or simply about enhancing existing goals within the client organization, it is difficult to make a 'shared model' work with many different parties. In the former case of a project-based collaboration, this is much simpler to create, and more common. Nevertheless, where the collaboration is more akin to the extension of an internal function or division, multi-party collaborations have substantive barriers to achieving three-way trust, and to agreeing common information sharing.

Risk of failure

Capability-based collaborations can cover a very wide spectrum – from bringing in a new technology to the production line, to a skills-based relationship via a corporate function. However, customarily the risk of failure is higher than a supply chain collaboration, but less than either a proposition-based or competitive collaboration. This is because there are positive benefits that result from collaborations of this nature, but often limited downside risks.

If the R&D collaboration fails to find that new drug, the firms have lost the costs of their investment, but that is all. Customers were not affected, market share was not lost and existing revenue did not decline. This tends to be the case because the focus of this type of collaboration is on enhancement. If that extra performance, in whatever area, is not achieved, it is disappointing for the organizations involved, but often not catastrophic.

Importance of cultural fit

For the project-based model of capability-based collaboration, cultural fit is very important, and actually relatively simple to attain. Any project, whether within an organization or across its boundaries, have some key characteristics that enable fit to happen. They are goal focused, time specific and bring together a group of people and resources to achieve a specific aim. Typically they do that in one location. These factors, particularly if some basic team orientation and team-building tools are used, mean fit can happen rapidly, even if the starting point is quite disparate.

For the ongoing model, fit is important because the collaboration partner is acting very much as that 'extended organization', and the definition of required cultural fit is at exactly the same level as deemed necessary between two functions in the same organization.

COMMERCIAL STRUCTURE

On most capability-based collaborations, the first and most important issue on the commercial agenda is that of Intellectual Property Rights (IPR). Not just the IPR that the collaboration hopes to bring about, but also the existing IPR that the parties are bringing to the table at the outset. Often a collaboration party has been chosen because they own IPR of real value; but who can use that, how can they use it and what if they share it? Closely linked to the IPR debate will be the commercial confidentiality expectations of each party, relating to both this IPR and the development the collaboration will do that builds from its base.

The discussions about IPR have often shaped the overall governance structure of the collaboration. If the IPR is 'leased' to the collaboration, but not to the 'host' company, then it is not uncommon for a legal entity to be formed to allow that transfer to happen. Collaboration partners often feel more comfortable if the developed IPR belongs to a legal entity that they have ownership of (normally partial), rather than using company-to-company contracts to try and control this issue. We have already discussed the challenge of defining the scope of a capability-based collaboration from a business sense – imagine the challenge from a legal perspective. Thus, putting all the activities into a new legal entity is a neat way of contractually defining scope, and also prevents potential future conflict. The differences between project and on-going collaborations need to be considered.

Project-based collaboration

Project-based collaborations benefit from the added simplicity of their time-based nature. The logic of their creation is that a particular goal can be achieved by combining resources from two or more organizations, rather than one organization trying to achieve the goal on its own. Given this nature, the goals can be defined relatively easily as well, and the expectations for time frame and cost agreed.

The most common commercial model in this instance is either a legal entity to house the project (less common), or a contractual agreement that confirms the cost, time, resource expectations of each party against the project goals. Normally, a joint board is created across the participating firms, which meets to review the progress against the stated goals, and makes decisions on variations.

The critical legal mechanisms to put in place concern the funding of the collaboration – whether financial or resource-based. Taking the R&D example, who pays if the first clinical trial is unsuccessful and the drug formulae has to be redeveloped? Due to the fact that initially these items are unknown, and scope will be a managed process not an upfront definition, a commercial structure is required to run back-to-back with the scope process. What can be agreed are the principles of doing this. How are overrun costs shared? How and when can parties decide if they wish to stop the collaboration because it is taking longer or costing more than planned? And of course, on a more positive note, if the collaboration achieves its goals underbudget, how is this saving shared? Finally, if the model includes a sharing of marketplace success, how also does over-achievement work here?

'On-going' collaboration

Given the typical two-way nature of capability-based collaborations and the fact that there tends to be a 'dominant' party, the real question concerning commercial and governance models is 'What is the main point of collaboration control?' Does the main party wish to purchase the capability, and then attempt to direct that to achieve goals; does it wish to set goals and allow the partner to utilize whatever resource it sees fit to achieve them; does it wish to set a budget and get the most it can for the money? For example, consider the capability to create and manage a brand. The dominant party could say:

☐ 'Here's $10 million – do as much as you can for that.'

☐ 'Give me an eight person team for six months and let's see what we can do.'

☐ 'I want 60 per cent brand name recognition with socio-economic group ABC1 by the end of June – what will that cost me?'

Answering the question posed will lay out the path for how the commercial deal will be structured. Note that performance risk sits at very different points in each of these three example questions. Bear in mind an appropriate governance approach, and how financial rewards and collaboration funding should flow between the parties involved.

PLANNING TOOLS

Developing the goals, scope and structure for a capability-based collaboration can be greatly assisted by a set of appropriate and proven tools. For this collaboration model, the most commonly used techniques are:

☐ **Gating templates** – To manage progress where new concepts are being developed, but visibility is required along the way.

☐ **Contribution analysis** – To assist in understanding where and how the collaboration contributes to outputs that are of interest to shareholders and other stakeholders.

☐ **Competency analysis** – To identify and manage the competencies which the collaboration is bringing and to use this for broader use.

Each of these three key tools can bring clarity, focus and enable common understanding.

Gating templates

Many capability-based collaborations are about new things: new product or service development; innovative production technologies; original brand or marketing mechanisms. The challenge is that you will not know until it is too late, whether the investments you make in these areas will pay off. Only when the new product has been launched will you know if it works; and to get to that point you may have evaluated 100 possibilities. With 40 different brand ideas on the table, which two do you pick, and will they work for you?

Gating templates allow a number of things to be managed:

☐ They add specific review points to the development process to screen out unlikely prospects before too much investment is spent.

☐ They define clear criteria, based on output success, around which reviews can be conducted.

☐ They allow for, based on the scoring against criteria, a forecast of expected performance once the development item has reached completion. This is compared to whatever goal metrics were defined for the collaboration.

☐ They provide the basis for reporting to the collaboration board on the progress of the collaboration.

☐ They compile the total list of development items into definable phased groups, so that the 'pipeline' is visible.

Contribution analysis

Contribution analysis brings a similar philosophy to collaborations as that used by organizations in areas such as, Shareholder Value Analysis (SVA) or Economic Value Added (EVA). While it can have applications across all collaboration models, it is of particular use in capability-based collaborations. This is due to the difficulty of linking their role to output success, and because the types of activities that a capability-based collaboration can focus on is almost limitless.

The starting point for contribution analysis is within the dominant partner, not the collaboration. The key strategic targets of that organization need to be understood and defined. These may be EPS (earnings per share) growth, EVA, return on capital employed (ROCE) or market share growth. Starting from a strategic target, the key drivers that comprise it are defined. If, for example, the key metric was ROCE, the level one drivers would be revenue, cost of goods, other costs, profits, fixed assets, working capital and so on. Each of these level one drivers would then be broken down into level two drivers. Therefore, revenue may break down into number of customers, average order value, order frequency and churn. Each of these could then be analyzed to third or fourth level drivers. Once the driver map is complete, we can start considering collaboration contribution.

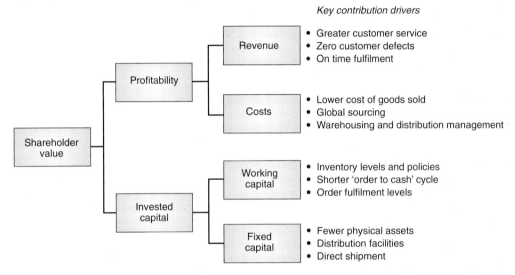

FIGURE 3.1: Contribution analysis

The lowest level drivers can be assessed to consider whether the activities of the collaboration can impact these strategic priorities. At first, a straightforward high, medium or low assessment can set the scene. When it is clear where to focus, the contribution can be considered in a more quantified way, until every area in which the collaboration contributes to the strategic aspiration can be evaluated, quantified and consolidated. This framework serves as the ongoing method to review the contribution of the collaboration to the overall organization.

Competency analysis

Human competencies are core to most capability-based collaborations. These comprise the skills and abilities of the individuals that collectively represent an organizational capability. Having a tool to assess, monitor and manage this area is very useful. Thankfully, competencies can use a structure, which is as formal as the process analysis, to articulate what they are and how they improve. A typical competency model identifies competency under three headings:

1 **Intent** – What are the personal characteristics?

2 **Action** – What are the skills that demonstrate those characteristics?

3 **Outcome** – How do these actions deliver role performance?

In all areas, competency analysis identifies statements, which define 'what good looks like'.

Intent will focus on the motives, traits and knowledge of the individual. For example, organizations may wish individuals to have the motive of action-orientation, and the way that this is observed may be that 'Motivated people consistently set challenging goals for themselves, take personal responsibility to accomplish them, and use feedback to the better.' A trait considers the physical characteristics that may be needed; reaction time and good eyesight could be an example for a combat pilot. Knowledge is about learned facts and information, for instance, a surgeon's knowledge of the nerves and muscles in the human body. Although knowledge delivers no direct contribution, it is the enabler that allows skills to deliver value.

Skill, quite simply, is the ability to perform a physical or mental task. For example, a computer programmer's ability to organize 50,000 lines of code in a sequential order. It is these sets of skills that ultimately allow performance outcomes, such as quality, productivity, new products or services, to be achieved. Competency analysis allows for each of these elements to be defined and assessed. A strategy is then created which either outlines how competency will be developed within the collaboration to enhance its ability to deliver goals, or how that capability can be passed to participating organizations for longer term value.

OPERATING MODEL

While clarity of goals and scope is the starting point, and putting in place the necessary commercial and governance structures an essential precursor, how does a capability collaboration operate on a day-to-day basis?

Physical location

Unlike supply chain collaboration where location is a key indicator of cost, its role is less direct for capability collaborations. Capability collaborations involve the sharing of skills, knowledge, competency and resource to achieve stated goals. Location decisions should be made with this in mind. If people are based together is this interplay helped? Which parts of the collaboration's activities require staff from multiple organizations to work together and where is it more self-contained? For ongoing collaborations, support of cultural fit and team-working will provide the answer. For project-based collaborations co-location is almost always the logical answer. Creating the energy around a single goal output, delivered by one team of people is almost always easier when people physically sit together.

The most common barrier to these principles of location is where sites hold complex or expensive equipment. Moving an R&D facility may be a logistical impossibility. The other constraints are where IPR agreements mean that some resources need to be ring-fenced by one party in the relationship. However, at a conceptual level, put projects together; use location as a lever to create shared ownership for ongoing collaborations.

Points of interface

If the nature of the collaboration dictates that interfaces are managed across the organizational interface (e.g. in the case of two departments within a company), then the same extended organization principles described under the supply chain collaboration model apply. The alternative model, frequently the case for capability-based collaborations is when joint teams, involving staff from each party, are working together to develop or deliver the stated outputs. Here the point of interface is a continuous one, and necessary actions must be put in place to make this effective. Manage the process of team creation (roles, operating model), create a common set of values which defines how the unit will behave and set clear authority levels for both spend and decision making that are consistent regardless of organizational home. Finally, where possible, agree common terms and conditions around working hours and benefits.

Place of belonging and development

A project-based collaboration is clearly the place where individuals should feel their first 'home' is for its duration. This means that the project structure needs to allow for line management that provides coaching, development and feedback, and that a social agenda is part of the overall plan. For continuous collaborations, the split over place of belonging is the same as for points of interface. Where the collaboration capability is provided by one party, then the principles for supply chain collaborations apply. However, where success is achieved through a collective, multi-organization operating entity, then that entity must be the place where those participating in the collaboration feel they belong.

To belong somewhere means the entity must have an identity of its own. Give consideration to items such as:

☐ Creating a brand or name for the entity.

☐ Creating a 'sense' of what that entity stands for. This could be everything from formal values statements, through to simple things like developing new PC templates for all documents produced by the collaboration.

☐ Specifically choosing operating areas where a different approach to that of the parent companies' model is applied. This could be as simple as the meeting management process or as complex as the reporting format or employment contract.

☐ Focusing on what the collaboration gives to the individual and dedicate disproportionate time and resource to that area. For example, if it is about knowledge and learning, providing clear mechanisms to provide that.

Role of technology

We can recognize that a particular capability-based collaboration may be one where the capability delivered is technology-based. However, consider generally what role technology plays to operate capability collaborations. We are not particularly focused on process activities and steps and therefore technology used for automation and integration will be of less value (e.g. like the ERP backbone). As a rule, the collaboration will not be engaging directly with the customer community and so CRM is not going to be of much value. Instead, capability is more about knowledge-based systems and information provision. It is these tools that tend to be of greater priority.

Capability-based collaborations need mechanisms to access information, often from the parent organizations, and then to develop and share learning within the collaboration. Portal technology is often the mechanism used to access information because it can be quickly put in place, draws from legacy systems or otherwise, and can be entity-neutral. Knowledge systems often need to be uniquely structured to reflect the goal of the collaboration itself, and particularly if it is a new entity that comprises staff from all participating organizations working together. However, where the collaboration is about sourcing a capability that acts as an extension to an internal organizational unit, the in-house systems can also extend to provide the common operating platform.

Method of incentives

The model and the need for incentive alignment is directly answered by the choice of commercial and governance model. If we return to the three possible ways to work with a brand agency, each one dictates an incentive model:

- ☐ If the commercial model is 'achievements for $10 million', then individuals should have incentives to achieve the plan that was agreed. It is milestone-based.

- ☐ If the commercial model is to provide a team of eight, then the individuals should be kept on whatever incentive scheme the parent company has to motivate skilled individuals within its field.

- ☐ If the commercial model is to 'achieve 60 per cent brand recognition', then a team-based scheme, which links personal gain to that output goal is required.

For each of these three scenarios, whether that incentive model needs to be aligned across organizations, or within one party depends on which of the two collaboration models is deployed – project-based or ongoing.

COMMON PITFALLS

Capability-based collaboration is probably the 'loosest' model to both define and operate and many of the most common pitfalls are a direct result of this. The key ones to watch out for are:

- ☐ **Consider funding formulae** – Because the activities of a capability-based collaboration are likely to change over time in order to meet their stated goals, be clear at the beginning how funding will work amongst the respective parties to avoid conflict later.

- ☐ **Create a process for scope** – If scope cannot be agreed upfront, it is critical that a process is put in place to manage it on an ongoing basis, and that the commercial relationship directly links into this process.

- ☐ **Manage IPR commitments** – Often those working within the collaboration are clear on IPR and confidentiality agreements signed by the various parties. However, as these deliverables flow back into the 'host' organization they often touch individuals who are less aware. It is critical that all staff are fully briefed on the corporate obligations made in this area.

- ☐ **Focus on collaboration reporting** – Since the outputs of the collaboration are difficult to measure, and often take some time to come to fruition, measurement and reporting must be seen as even more important, rather than less so.

SUMMARY

1 Capability-based collaborations need to set the application of the capability to achieve a desired outcome as the goal and not the capability itself.

2 There are two clear types of capability-based collaboration: one-off project-based models and those that exist for ongoing operation.

3 Scope is hard to define within a capability-based collaboration. This should be linked to the goals and bounded by clear decisions on activities, costs and resource. Given that scope will change over time, scope management is an ongoing process which must be managed by the collaboration board and supported by the commercial model.

4 Focus the commercial and governance structures on clearly understanding ownership and management of both IPR and confidentiality.

5 Provide focus on the added value of a capability-based collaboration by clearly building a model using contribution analysis. Use that as the starting point to develop clear measurements for monitoring performance.

CHAPTER 4

PROPOSITION-BASED COLLABORATION

GOALS AND SCOPE

Before considering how to operate a proposition-based collaboration, it is critical to answer the question, 'Does this collaboration exist to create new propositions, or to execute an existing proposition?' If the answer is to create new propositions, the right model of collaboration is a capability-based one. If there is not yet a clear marketplace goal to execute, organizations are not being brought together to take a proposition to the marketplace, rather capability is pooled to try and develop one or more new propositions. The way that relationship needs to be managed is entirely different. It could be that the same parties move from operating as a capability-based collaboration to a proposition-based collaboration once they have developed that goal. However, to set the parameters clearly first, proposition-based collaborations exist once a clear marketplace offering has been developed and their role is then to execute that concept.

Given this context, the creation of goals for proposition-based collaborations are far simpler to devise. They require the proposition to be translated into targets for success. Often targets may be items such as market share, growth rates, cross-sell achievement, or even revenue or gross margin contribution.

As an example, take the collaboration that was trialled in the the late 1990s by Tesco and Marks & Spencer. Tesco were, at the time, almost exclusively a food retailer, and Marks & Spencer a clothes retailer. Each was considering extending into the other's domain, and instead chose to trial a 'dual store' concept. Purpose-built locations housed a major outlet for both organizations, which shared facilities. This gave customers easy access from one to the other – even to the point of allowing a single set of trolleys to be used around both stores. The proposition was simple to articulate and the measures of success equally transparent. Did either Tesco or Marks & Spencer generate greater sales by offering a combined proposition than they would expect from stores of that size if they were independent? In other words, was footfall higher, and were sales per square metre higher? Goals are fairly easy to define, and because we are referring to marketplace propositions, they can almost always be translated into dollars – whether revenue, margin, profit or a ratio. The critical factor, however, is that to define goals, we must be absolutely clear on scope. To be precise, what is the proposition?

The value mechanism

Taking a new value proposition (i.e. the description of benefits being provided to a customer in a given product or service 'bundle') to the market requires three things to be clearly understood:

1 **Defining the value proposition** – What sets of benefits are delivered to the customer, which customer segment is targeted, and how do these benefits translate to the actual product and service mix provided?

2 **Communicating the value proposition** – How and who is going to tell the marketplace about the arrival of this new proposition? Is there a brand associated with it, which company or companies will front it, what channels will it be sold through, and what market communications mechanisms will be used to do that?

3 **Delivering the value proposition** – There needs to be a value delivery system that fulfils the marketplace promise. That delivery mechanism will involve people, facilities, infrastructure, technology, information and many other elements. Who owns them, who manages them and who ensures that they do in fact deliver the proposition goals?

The crucial question is whether the collaboration is doing one, two or all three of these component parts. Does it exist to simply bring together the three to four organizations necessary to make the proposition happen, but all 'real work' is allocated out and executed in the home organizations? Or is it at the other extreme, where effectively a whole new business is created with its own sales, marketing, operations and support functions to take this proposition to the market, service the customer base and build a brand?

To enable us to create a structure and utilize tools to approach this model of collaboration, let us consider the three most common options that firms take along this potential scope continuum:

1 **The decision-making option** – Where the collaboration essentially combines key decision makers from each of the participating organizations who agree the strategy, identify the actions necessary to achieve them, and then allocate those to be executed by functions within the home organizations of each organization. Occasional cross-company project teams are created for specific tasks where necessary. A good example of this is where the GPS satellite system and major car manufacturers like Ford or General Motors combined elements of their businesses to create in-car navigation. Ford is never going to run a satellite network, and GPS are not going to start building cars; yet collaboration enabled this new proposition to come to the marketplace.

2 **The sales and marketing option** – This comprises all the elements of the decision-making option, and in addition an entity is formed, staffed by the participating firms to focus on managing the 'front-end' of the delivery. Typically this will consist of the marketing aspects to take the proposition to the targeted customer group and a sales force to generate and process orders. Fulfilment and service sits with the home organizations. Almost any of the dot.coms or NetMarkets (electronic trading places) fall into this

category. An organization which develops the route to market for the proposition, while the core operational capability of the parent organizations actually delivers the product or service to the customer.

3 **The whole entity option** – An entirely new legal entity is created to take the proposition to the marketplace, which manages all aspects of the delivery of the promise. The creation of the National Lottery in the UK is a clear example of this option. Created from a number of consortium partners, an entirely new entity called Camelot was formed to take this new proposition to the marketplace and manage all elements of its delivery.

KEY DRIVERS

We have defined the goals of the collaboration, and outlined three scope options, but what are the key drivers of this new collaboration model?

Scope of activity

Scope of activity is the fundamental difference between proposition-based collaborations and both capability-based and supply chain models. This is regardless of which of the three options of decision making, sales and marketing or whole entity are picked. By definition, a proposition-based collaboration offers something that increases the scope of activity of the participating organizations. If scope has not increased, then it cannot be a new proposition. Recognizing that we are talking about new scope immediately presents a challenge – this is uncharted water. We may not know how to measure success, we certainly cannot accurately predict whether the proposition will be well received by the market and, as organizations working together, we are in activity areas that are new for all of us, even if drawing from expertise in areas we know well.

Focus of collaboration

The focus of the collaboration, almost by definition, will be marketplace. It is about providing customers with a new proposition, which gives them more benefit. As such, it will be marketplace measurements that define its success. In simple terms, this is some form of penetration measure – market share, share of wallet or revenue growth. However, most commonly the purpose of the value proposition is to build a differentiated offer, where the test of success is not only about volume, but also unit price. Differentiated offers deliver a high benefit mix that should, in turn, lead to the organization being able to charge premium price for that added value. Often, therefore, the focus of the collaboration, and the measure of its true success, is the ability to sustain a price premium against similar competing offers in the marketplace.

Typical number of parties

For proposition-based collaboration, there are no obvious rules of thumb about how many parties will make it successful. The offer around which the collaboration is built can be so varied that each will dictate its own membership. When the oil and gas industry gathered 17 of the largest players to create an industry exchange, this was an appropriate number because this trading proposition needed liquidity and a commitment of spend. Similarly with most other exchanges or NetMarkets. When AT&T and BT wanted to create a transatlantic service for large corporates in the telecommunications space, which they did through the invention of Concert, two was an appropriate number. Proposition-based collaborations can be anything from two to 20, entirely dependent on the type and nature of the offer provided.

Risk of failure

Risk is a critical, if not the critical, driver that needs to be considered in the creation and management of proposition-based collaborations. The level of risk changes depending on which of the three options – decision making, sales and marketing or whole entity – is chosen, but all carry a high degree of risk, both upside and downside.

Financial consequences are not the only risk. When major corporations come together and claim they have brought something new to the market, there are high levels of executive and corporate ego that go with it. Backing out of a high profile proposition-based collaboration and admitting failure, tends to be career destructive for individuals, and often financial suicide for organizations.

Therefore, how does risk get managed? Sometimes it just cannot be managed. One route is to move towards a whole entity model by starting at a decision making one. As success shows itself, move through the other options. However, this tends to mitigate downside risk by increasing upside risk. Delivering a new proposition through existing organizations and not the collaboration, is strewn with operational and cultural barriers – the likelihood of success is less. A whole entity model makes it far more probable that the organization will succeed.

Instead, proposition-based collaborations are often best considered as a portfolio game. Many firms will have six to ten of these on the move at any time, with a clear expectation that some will fail. The upside win of a proposition-based collaboration is normally material. If a new proposition hits the marketplace and succeeds, the ROI will typically exceed the firm's ROCE enormously. Hence, risk needs to be considered at a corporate level and in a portfolio way, rather than at the collaboration level. Clearly, a risk management process is required for the collaboration, but if the question is 'Do I or do I not risk $100 million on this new venture?', risk managing that down to $95 million does not solve the issue.

Importance of cultural fit

Here, the choice of option is absolutely critical. With the decision-making option, cultural fit is irrelevant. What is important, is that the small group of executives who have put the concept together have, often at an individual-to-individual level, a degree of personal trust and corporate commitment to one another. That is very different to cultural fit. Two organizations that have absolutely no cultural fit can deliver a hugely successful proposition-based collaboration if two or three executives in each organization can 'get it together' and drive it through.

At the other end with the whole entity option, the question is not really about fit. We are considering a completely new organization that will create for itself a vision, brand, strategy, structure and *modus operandi*. Fit matters, but it is an absolute base necessity. And as for the middle ground – the sales and marketing option – the same rules apply as for capability-based collaboration. Where the collaboration works together, cultural fit is key; where it interfaces back into parent organizations, it is about making sure that the points of contact work effectively and deliver what they need to.

COMMERCIAL STRUCTURE

Commercial structure is king when it comes to proposition-based collaboration. There are many good reasons why that must be:

☐ Proposition-based collaborations typically create IPR, and often new brands and other trademarked items. These carry value on their own, are saleable, and their ownership needs clear agreement. This is far more challenging than in the situation of capability-based collaborations because usually the new intellectual property does not exist at the point of creation.

☐ Typically the 'power' behind the new entity is the marketing muscle flexed by the parent companies. In other words, the parent companies use their brands as collateral for the new entity. If Mars and Coca-Cola got together to create something new and marketed the entity as such, they are effectively promising that the Mars and Coca-Cola values stand behind this new offering. If that new offering fails – the impact on the parent brand can be devastating.

☐ Downside risk is high. There are hundreds of examples to show that billion dollar tags can sometimes be attached to major corporate failures in this area. When pain is felt at that level, it is amazing how quickly all corporate memories that are not recorded at the lawyer's office are swiftly forgotten.

In this model, the commercial contract between each party is critical. It needs to be considerate of who shares and owns upside prize. Many firms embark on proposition-based collaborations hoping to invent the new Microsoft or Cisco. Does the contract explain what would happen if this should occur? And of course, if it does, what exactly is the real value? Is it the brand of the new organization, a piece of technology it patents, the channel it creates to the marketplace or the trading assets of the business? Understanding how each of these elements is shared and owned is critical. Clearly, if it is a whole entity approach and a separate legal entity exists, often the argument is about dividing the share capital. However, even in this instance, being explicit about whether the resources put in place at the beginning of the collaboration by the participating organizations are legally transferred, leased or made available to use is a necessary exercise that will pay dividends later.

What if it goes wrong? Then, there are usually two issues to consider. How easily can a party withdraw, and who picks up the tab if it all fails? Exit strategy is a key area for each party to think through – both theirs and their partner's – even during the exhilaration of setting up the new collaboration and the exuberance of what it could bring to the market. Many telecommunications and media sector companies since 2000, have rued the day they signed exit deals as part of new collaborations where another partner could exit and they were forced to purchase their stake at a pre-agreed price. In the current market this is an unbelievable overpayment. Having options to acquire when the market is booming, turns into an enormous millstone when the market goes into free-fall. The only real way to consider this issue effectively is through the use of scenario planning, which needs to evaluate both good and bad markets; collaboration success and failure; and individual partner performance contribution. What would happen to the UK National Lottery if the terminals had never worked? Does everyone share the pain or could the other partners walk out? For each option, clear agreement needs to be given for both upside and downside risk, and upside and downside benefits.

Failure is bad enough – investments are written off, cash is drained, corporate ego takes a bruising and the operation is closed down. However, that might not be the end of it. What if the collaboration caused damage, either to the customer base, the market at large or to an individual partner? If the terminals for the National Lottery had not worked, it would not have meant only writing off the investment cost, it would have incurred a large bill from the

British Government for breach. Who picks that up? Or what about a NetMarket or one of the airline alliances, which is later deemed to have behaved in an anti-competitive way. Not only do competition commissions hand out nine or ten-figure fines, but every other player in that industry who has been wronged starts a queue outside the state court. Who pays? How is it shared? A legal team that understands all aspects of liability management will be worth their weight in gold, and needs to be brought into the process at the start.

And what of governance?

Having nailed the contract, how do we govern? For proposition-based collaboration, the most important principle is that of clear individual accountability. If the route taken is a whole entity option, it is very simple – all the usual governance structures of an operating company are needed. For the other options of decision making and sales and marketing, the small group of executives who have agreed upon a strategy must be equally clear about who is accountable for what. There is little shared responsibility – it is more about each bringing their part of the jigsaw puzzle to make sure that the whole picture is built.

PLANNING TOOLS

Proposition-based collaborations are about three things – an ability to assess and monitor market opportunity, an ability to evaluate and manage proposition delivery, and the clarity of accountability to operate the collaboration. There is a proven tool, which can support the collaboration in each of these areas:

☐ **Market value analysis** – To assess the benefits that target customers seek from a particular product or service area, and whether they would pay a premium for that service.

☐ **Value proposition evaluation** – To provide a tool to monitor whether the intended value proposition is delivered to customers.

☐ **Accountability matrices** – To ensure that there is a clear mechanism around which consensus can be gained, regarding responsibility and accountability for delivery.

Each of these three key tools can bring clarity, focus and enable common understanding.

Market value analysis

Organizations attempt to identify customer needs by using market research generally. This uses techniques focused most often around 'features' of products and services. How quickly would you like the telephone answered? How accurate do you want your bills to be? What sort of lead time would you like on your delivery? What functionality does the product need to have? Proposition development, however, requires a focus on benefits, not functions, and these are related to what the customer's organization does, not to what our organization offers. Market value analysis attempts to answer this question.

The process to drive out benefits requires a cross-functional, cross-company workshop with key customers in the target group. The workshop, which typically requires one to two days, would follow these key steps:

☐ Identify who the customers' target customers or segments are.

☐ Identify what product and service mix these customers have (i.e. what is the customer's value proposition?).

☐ Understand how the customer is trying to differentiate to its customers.

☐ Map out the customer's process, and identify within those processes the critical activities that are performed, which deliver the differentiation aspiration of the customer (i.e. what is the customer's value delivery system?).

☐ Identify where your organization inputs to the customer's process.

☐ Map out your organization's processes, which lead to the inputs provided for the customer's process.

☐ Jointly discuss opportunities to better align your processes to the client's.

☐ Summarize those needs in a set of benefits statements that articulate the client requirement (e.g. 'easy to contact', 'stock always on the racking in the production facility'), rather than product or service features.

Value proposition evaluation

Typically, organizations monitor elements, such as customer satisfaction or customer loyalty, as a yardstick for considering success. However, a collaboration exists solely to deliver a specific proposition to the marketplace and, therefore, understanding whether the offer is indeed being received by customers is necessary. A tool for value proposition evaluation can provide this and it contains two parts:

1 Using market value analysis. Re-running benefit workshops with customers who helped to develop the proposition to test that the delivered service they are receiving does indeed close the benefit gaps.

2 Using benefit monitoring as an ongoing mechanism.

Benefit monitoring takes the benefit statements and turns them into standards, around which the value delivery system is built. Thus, while 'easy to deal with' may be the benefit, it needs to be translated into a set of product and service elements, which together deliver this promise. This could be:

☐ Making multiple ordering mechanisms (web, phone, face to face, post) available.

☐ Having two-ring pick up in the call centre, with number recognition and customer named answering.

☐ Putting full customer history into the hands of all customer-facing staff, whether call centre operators or field service agents.

☐ Redesigning the bill statement to ease understanding.

☐ Proactively informing customers of the status of orders.

For each value delivery element, a measure can be created. Those measures that together comprise a benefit can be monitored against targets, and an overall benefit delivery summary produced.

Accountability matrices

Although straightforward as a tool, proposition-based collaborations fail time after time because the effort has not been made to make roles and responsibilities clear. The RACI (Responsibility Accountability Consulted Informed) tool enables this to be done. It not only covers roles and responsibility, but also allows communication issues to be considered. The elements of RACI are:

- ☐ **Responsibility** – Who carries out the action?

- ☐ **Accountability** – Who has the yes/no decision regarding that action and where does the 'buck stop'?

- ☐ **Consulted** – Who should be involved in advance of the decision being made or the action being executed?

- ☐ **Informed** – Who needs to be told after the event that the action or decision has happened?

A simple matrix can be built with every area of the collaboration down one side, and each of the parties within the collaboration along the other. In each box on the matrix an R, A, C or I can be placed. It is important that for any item, there is only one accountability assigned – the 'buck' cannot stop twice. Furthermore, many organizations struggle with the concept of splitting the accountability from the responsibility. However, the person who decides and the person who does, can be different and in many situations are.

OPERATING MODEL

The operating model for the collaboration will vary widely, depending on which of the three options we are considering. In this section we will contrast decision making with whole entity. For sales and marketing, it is better to consider the capability-based collaboration as a model. Guidance for that area can be found in Chapter 3.

Physical location

For decision making this is clear. Stay separate. The decision-making model is an approach based around organizations managing their own operations independent, around a marketplace promise. Beyond each party knowing their role in the overall game plan, being together is unnecessary and unhelpful. The only occasion where this rule may need to be reconsidered is if the market perception of the new proposition could be damaged. Recognizing that proposition-based collaboration is about a market offer, on occasion a front office for the offer is needed to give credibility and perceived independence in the eyes of current and prospective customers. Typically, if this is needed, it is in the form of a sales or executive office building, rather than housing an operational capability.

Where a whole entity model is used, location is critical. It is the starting point for creating the new identity for the organization. The collaboration should use premises that do not belong to the parent organizations if possible – a Greenfield site is ideal – and it should be located on neutral ground. All staff relating to the new organization need to work together in the location or locations, and begin to form the values and operating method that best support the market offer.

Points of interface

The decision-making options almost invariably involve either executive or senior management interface. The collaboration requires individuals who can commit material resources from their organizations to the collaboration strategy. Thus, the points of interface do not tend to be departmental-based, but rather individual role and personality-driven. To make these effective, the need is not so much for organizational clarity, service level agreements and so on, but instead for personal trust, integrity and straight talking. This certainly needs to be backed up by corporate commitment, but fundamentally individuals make the decision-making option happen.

For the whole entity approach, there are no interfaces to manage from an organizational point of view; everyone who delivers the proposition works for that organization.

Place of belonging and development

There is a challenging dilemma to find the place that people working in the collaboration call home. The whole entity option is simple – the collaboration is their new home. They need employment contracts issued by that organization, they need to be legally transferred so that a single set of HR policies and processes supports all staff in the entity regardless of their historic home, and their loyalty needs to be aligned to the named collaboration, not to its parent owners. However, what of decision-making collaborations?

Surely, the immediate response is that the place of belonging is the parent company? The collaboration really only exists in the eyes of the market – it is not an actual entity in the operational sense. Nevertheless, if you examine the behaviours of the core executive group, which bring a proposition-based collaboration into being, they often feel a far greater sense of belonging and ownership of that creation, than they do towards their employing organization – it is their 'baby'. The question to ask is whether this is appropriate, and the answer is to consider risk and regression. If the collaboration fails, will that lead to the end of the relationship between the executive and his or her employing organization? Is the collaboration a career gamble, where both parties recognize that the individual's future is inextricably linked to whether the collaboration succeeds or not? Although this may seem harsh, the cost of failure is often so great that it is an inevitable consequence. Evidently, the prize for success is equally dramatic. If the collaboration succeeds, it is appropriate that the core executive group moves personal affiliation to the new creation. However, if they are there to represent their parent organizations, they need to remain loyal to their paying owner.

Role of technology

In the whole entity model, technology has exactly the same role as in any organization. Often collaborations will lever either technology templates from parent organizations, or as a minimum take advantage of purchase deals. Nevertheless, broadly it needs an IT strategy and execution method like any normal business. For most, IT is outsourced from day one, in part to assist downside risk mitigation.

With regards to the decision-making option, technology is almost entirely irrelevant. The only critical component is to have shared measurement and reporting data, and for that a simple business warehouse and presentation interface is necessary. These are small and simple investments compared to that required, for example, by supply chain collaboration.

Method of incentives

The nature of proposition-based collaboration means that it is common for incentives, particularly for decision making, to be focused around value creation in a very real sense – shareholder value. Where the core group of executives has created the new concept, their reward is typically based around option holding in an appropriate legal entity. If the price for failure is leaving the company, the upsides need to equally reflect that personal risk. If reward is through another mechanism – either a bonus or Long Term Incentive Plan (LTIP), it is normally firmly linked to actual profit or equity appreciation of the collaboration.

The pay and incentive theories that apply to any organization can be used for the whole entity option, however, it is noticeable that organizations of this nature tend to focus more on equity ownership amongst staff, than their parent companies do. This typically reflects both the entrepreneurial spirit they are trying to create, and recognizes the shared risk taken by all parties.

COMMON PITFALLS

Proposition-based collaboration has different characteristics compared to any of the other collaboration models. Making it work can be helped by considering the following:

☐ **Risk approach** – Recognize that risk is high in this model, and that to try and mitigate it at the collaboration level is often impossible. Indeed, attempting to do that often leads to collaborations never getting off the ground. It is better to consider this at a corporate level and to have a portfolio game. Having only just one or two proposition collaborations, if they each carry high risk, is inadvisable.

☐ **Choose an option** – Collaboration structure in this model can contain many shades of grey. We have outlined three options and it is sensible to be clear which option your organization chooses to use.

☐ **Focus on the legals** – Contracts are paramount, and they demand focused time and money to be spent on them. The issue frequently is not about the investment risk never returning, but about the potential liability issues from partners and customers if the offer does not achieve the expected marketplace acceptance.

☐ **Use scenario planning** – Proposition-based collaborations are each, typically, a 'one shot deal'. It is key to effectively run the scenarios to consider market changes, partner performance issues and customer acceptance, and how to quantify the impact of each.

☐ **Be accountable** – Apart from the whole entity model, proposition-based collaboration mostly concerns each partner contributing his or her part to the overall picture. This means that accountability needs to be clearly agreed at the beginning, and a mechanism put in place to make partners accountable and to hold them accountable.

SUMMARY

1   Proposition-based collaborations exist to execute a new proposition, not to develop ideas for new propositions. If the latter is the goal, the capability-based collaboration model is the right tool to use.

2   The primary goals for any proposition-based collaboration will be marketplace oriented.

3   By definition, a proposition-based collaboration is creating something which is new in scope for all of the participating organizations. This means that it carries a high degree of uncertainty and risk.

4 Scope is critical and can be viewed along the three elements of the value proposition chain: development, communication and delivery. Three options for proposition-based collaboration therefore exist, which we have termed decision making, sales and marketing and whole entity.

5 The cost of failure, particularly downside risk, is very high, and so contract creation and management will be a key driver, including clarity of who will own the IPR developed by the collaboration.

6 Use the RACI tool to bring clarity to roles and responsibilities within the collaboration.

7 In general, for all options of proposition-based collaboration, the place of belonging is the collaboration.

CHAPTER 5

COMPETITIVE COLLABORATION

GOALS AND SCOPE

Better, faster, stronger, more competitive, higher value. These are all good goal statements for an organization, yet none of them are appropriate to apply to a competitive collaboration. Raw Porterian power is the card that gets a player to the collaboration table. In addition, having control of a route to the marketplace is the enabling key driver. Given that the carrot offered by such a firm is customer access, the goal is market share for almost every competitive collaboration.

For some, customer access carries an additional aspiration: a higher unit price. Take away choice or use customer inertia – if you can get your product or service to them more conveniently, they will not price test it. This secondary goal area can, at times, border on the sinister or come close to the boundaries of what is legal under the various anti-competitive legislation. This is a key topic discussed in this chapter.

There is greyness in places, between competitive collaboration and proposition-based collaboration – not in design, but in what the reality is versus the claims of organizations in the marketplace. Do the collaborations in the airline industry really bring a new proposition based around travel simplicity for the customer, or are groups of airlines trying to put each other out of business by taking dominant positions in constrained routes? Is it about a new value proposition, or is it really just a Porterian power game? While the receiving customer community may sit and ponder these questions, the organizations behind them clearly know the reality, and for them there is no doubt about which of the four collaboration models they should be using.

The goal in almost every competitive collaboration situation is market share increase and occasionally margin enhancement, but what about scope? Is it the same or different? For competitive collaboration there are two factors to consider:

1 Groups of customers, and the manner in which a player has unique control or access to them.

2 Sets of products and services which could be provided.

The scope of a competitive collaboration is all about deciding who matches what from the above factors. What is the mechanism for rewarding the cooperative party that allows their customer base to be accessed by your products and services?

In general, however the conclusion is reached, there is no increased scope for the participating organizations. The product and service are offered to a new customer group, or a customer group is approached in a different way. There is a slight overlap with proposition-based collaboration here where the commercial method is a 'tit for tat' reciprocal model: 'If you recommend my hotel chain to your customers, I'll recommend your car hire company to mine'. That is fine, and represents no increase in proposition and, therefore, no change in activity to either organization. However, sometimes this relationship is supported further by a new pricing proposition. For example, if you show your hotel room key to the car hire company, they will give you 10 per cent off. Or perhaps you get the car free for a weekend if you upgrade to an executive suite at the hotel. Fundamentally, though, there is no real change to what either company does – one still runs hotels, the other hires cars. Nevertheless, managing this combined 'proposition' can be seen as a minor increase on organizational scope.

This model of collaboration is commonplace: my customers, your products. At a simple level, McDonald's and Disney do it, Ford and Barclaycard do it and Tesco and Royal Bank of Scotland do it. Consider almost every airline, hotel chain, car hire company and holiday operator; they all have 'partners' that they align with to share opportunities and to hopefully gain access to a partially defended customer base. These examples sit only on the first step of the competitive scale.

Economic advantage

OPEC is the most famous, legal cartel in the world, which collectively controls one of the most valuable resources on the planet – black gold. The fundamentals of supply and demand are debated and managed in an open and visible way; the world's superpowers define the oil price they want and OPEC attempts to get the producing nations to manage output quotas to achieve that goal. The ability or otherwise of this governing body to be effective is well documented, and rogue nations have breached their quotas when national financial situations dictate it. However, this is an example where economic advantage to certain states and companies is achieved by totally controlling the route to market and the balance of supply and demand.

From the early 1990s, the trend towards globalization and industry consolidation has increased on a massive scale. In 1980, around 50 per cent of the world's GDP (Gross Domestic Product) was operating in an open trading environment – that figure has now exceeded 80 per cent. The mega-mergers, for instance, the creation of gsk, Vodafone's takeover of Mannessman and the organizations that formed the now colossal Citi group have led to the 'U'-shaped model in national industries applying globally. The U-shaped model refers to the shape of most industries if plotted on a graph according to revenue size – lots of small players, a few large players and very few in the middle. Where four or five players dominated a national market in the 1960s and 1970s, now four or five players dominate the global corporate arena – whether for oil exploration, telecommunications, financial services or information technology. And with this comes the opportunity for firms to truly gain economic advantage by collaborating, particularly in cross-industry arrangements, and to move power away from the primary producers in the value chain, and also back from the end customer themselves.

Collaboration models

We have talked about 'tit for tat' reciprocal models at the basic trading level, but what are the other ways to gain economic advantage through competitive collaboration? The acid test is 'How constrained is the customer group?' If Intel have persuaded Packard Bell to put one of their processors in the majority of PCs they build – the customer has no choice. The same end-user branding strategy is applied by many players further up the value chain, which ensures that their profit slice is protected. 'Big lever clubs' are groups within an industry value chain who get together and can exert much greater bargaining power over their suppliers. This has been seen in the electronic trading exchanges enabled by the internet revolution. Finally, there is the extreme example of the whole entity option applied to competitive collaboration, where controlling parent companies create legal entities that exist purely to enable the power card to be played. This situation has also been seen in the defence industry and in raw material production. Generally, once an industry reaches this end of the competitive scale, the next step is to merge or acquire; the line is crossed away from collaboration.

KEY DRIVERS

Competitive collaboration is clearly very different to all other forms of collaboration. It is not about improvement, it does not relate to customer satisfaction – it may even work against it. So, what are the key drivers that describe its make-up?

Scope of activity

In principle, competitive collaborations do not change the scope of activity of the participating firms. We have discussed the fact that new pricing options may provide a new proposition in the customer's eye, but that in core work architecture, capability and focus of the originating organizations, nothing has changed. If scope does begin to grow it is a good indicative sign that the operating model for forming the relationship is going beyond that of collaboration, towards one where either a formal joint venture or merger and acquisition is appropriate.

Focus of collaboration

Competitive collaboration is all about routes to market – the channel strategy – and so the goal will be about marketplace. However, because the scope of the business is unchanged and, therefore, so is the proposition, this is a focus on penetration and market share.

We have already mentioned a secondary agenda, where firms attempt to fundamentally change the supply and demand equation through this opportunity, either in reality or in perception. Where that is the case, the focus is somewhat different. If the end goal of the collaboration is to enable prices to either be kept high or to be pushed up, the focus is about explicitly attempting to remove power and choice from the customer and return it to the supplying company. The measure of achieving this is gross margin before and after the collaboration is formed.

Typical number of parties

Competitive collaboration can be considered to have two broad types. The first is the company-to-company reciprocal arrangement. Here firms either swap access to their respective customer bases, or they agree a commercial incentive when it looks like the partnership will be a one-way street. The second is where one step in an industry value chain collectively attempts to shift power. In any industry value chain, power will exist at different levels along it. For example, in food retailing, ten years ago the power sat with the food manufacturers because they were bigger and more powerful than the retailers. Over the past ten years the number of retailers has reduced, and the top five have become dominant and so stronger than the manufacturers. Power has shifted along the value chain. Today, using collaboration, this sort of shift could be achieved simply by the firms cooperating, rather than by consolidating the industry. The second model goes closest to the wind in terms of competition commissions, as Covisint (the NetMarket created in the automotive sector) found when the three leading American car manufacturers tried to join forces. Nevertheless, the value of achieving industry-wide purchasing power is evident.

The number of parties for competitive collaboration is often two or many, but rarely in between. In part, this is because this collaboration involves high stakes and leads to a high level of risk.

Risk of failure

Why are the stakes high? This is where we begin to understand that partnership and collaboration do not mean the same thing. Partnership implies working together for common benefit. Competitive collaboration explicitly pursues a win-lose strategy. In effect, if somebody loses, the risks go up. Your customers may recognize that you are trying to move the balance of power in order to drive your prices up. Your competitors could, once they understand the game that is being played, move aggressively in either a price war or through the courts. The business press likes nothing better than to hold up a well-known corporation and, more specifically its chief executive, and explain how a shady corporation-to-corporation deal was pursued for the good of 'corporate greed' against the needs of customers or the broader business community.

Importance of cultural fit

The good news about competitive collaboration is that cultural fit is completely irrelevant. This model of collaboration takes the decision-making option of proposition-based collaboration to the next level. It is not uncommon for these kind of collaborative arrangements to be purely a chief executive officer-to-chief executive officer affair in their creation. Competitive collaboration is about economic power and, therefore, cultural fit is not only unimportant, it should not figure on the agenda at all. Decision-making proposition-based collaborations do not require cultural fit, but they do need trust between a core group of executives. This is unnecessary, and sometimes dangerous, in competitive collaboration. Instead, the parties involved should be able to sit in the room, put themselves in the shoes of the opposing party, and consider whether the economic argument for the collaboration is absolutely compelling for all members. If the business case stacks up for the opposing party, and it stacks up for your party, then success is a real possibility.

COMMERCIAL STRUCTURE

In most competitive collaborations, the starting point of commercial consideration is not company-to-company, but at the office of the commission responsible for competition in the territory where the collaboration will operate. This may be the European Competition Directorate, its American counterpart or national anti-trust organizations. Some sectors, like telecommunications, ex-public sector markets, and those where power is seen to be too concentrated, have legislation in place to lay the framework. For others, general principles apply, but discretion always sits with the commissioner.

Understanding competition legislation is increasingly a corporate minefield, even for the best trained and most savvy team of advisors. This is partly because different countries are unbundling both the privatized industries and protectionist legislation at different rates. Furthermore, national and supra-national bodies have not always taken a common approach to this topic. This was starkly demonstrated by Europe and the US office taking opposing positions on what Jack Welch hoped would be his leaving present to the General Electric shareholders, the acquisition of Honeywell. To obtain as much visibility at the industry level is the starting point, when looking at the legal and commercial position.

Beyond that, legal consideration is facilitated by breaking competitive collaboration into the two options already described:

1   **Company-to-company** – Ranging from simple reciprocal deals, to larger tie ups between major industry players attempting to sow up particular customer groups.

2   **Industry groups** – As commonly seen through the online exchanges, but also outside the digital economy as well.

Company-to-company

These contracts tend to benefit from forward thinking. It is common for a company-to-company based competitive collaboration to be a testing ground that ultimately leads to an acquisition or merger. If this is a known possible future scenario, the manner in which the contract is put together will differ to two organizations that collaborate for mutual economic gain. Either way, the most important focus of the contractual considerations is usually the mechanisms and assumptions for sharing additional profits generated by the opening up of the respective customer bases. This can be particularly complex if it is a two-way exchange and, for example, if it is highly successful for one organization but a relative failure for the other. Is this mitigated upfront, or is it a 'try your luck' model? Considering the nature of this collaboration, the critical test is 'What happens if perceived economic advantage proves not to exist?'

Governance is equally simple for this model. Normally the deal-makers will meet at a sensible level of frequency to review whether the economic drivers expected at the beginning have materialized. They need to consider whether this implies a further alignment or the addition of another party into the collaboration, or indeed if success is elusive, whether a reversal is needed. For company-to-company relationships, because they are generally 'deal'-based – from a marketplace point of view the collaboration is not there one day and is the next – feedback on success is fairly swift. Moreover, the ability to benchmark against the pre-collaboration performance level is reasonably straightforward.

Industry group

For industry groups, the dynamics are entirely different. Typically, a dominant player is needed – a ringleader. This may be due to the economic power that a particular organization holds or frequently it can be about the vision or pure ambition of a particular individual that drives the agenda through. Collaborations that require a group to collectively agree a route forward need the focus of one individual in order to quickly attain critical mass.

Such ventures are usually discussed only at the upper echelons of the organization, sometimes the chief executives themselves, and therefore all of the challenges of corporate and personal ego come into play. In addition, hardened competitors may be sitting together in a room discussing the need to work together for the first time. Sometimes the same company you are collaborating with is also, in another sphere of your operation, your fiercest competitor.

Generally, where a competitive collaboration attempts to get a group of players together, two commercial and governance models result. The first is where a new entity is formed, often a not-for-profit one, collectively owned by the participating organizations. The second is where a third party is used to operate the 'industry entity' to provide a sense of marketplace independence. While this latter model carries some challenges, it does benefit from avoiding the daily operational problems of representatives from maybe ten companies that are attempting to build something together, where clearly different vested interests lie.

PLANNING TOOLS

With competitive collaboration, poker is a better synonym than partnership. The tools to help us think this issue through need to reflect this. Essentially, an ability to identify opportunities to shift power is needed. To then consider how customers and competitors will react to such actions, and to move key executives to a point where they are comfortable to put such deals in place is critical. Three tools can assist, one for each area.

The 'five forces' suite

Identifying the levers of power has never been better described than in Porter's model developed in the mid 1980s. Looking at each of the drivers that comprise buyer, supplier, and new entrant power against existing rivalry, provides the basis for examining how to shift power. However, there are broader tools than the basic model to apply. Collecting data on actual market share information by country or customer group, and using the competitive concentration ratio formula overlaid onto the Porter framework begins to quantify the evaluation. This ratio is also used routinely by the various competition commission authorities. Finally, within the 'suite' further quantification can be added by using PIMS data[1], which provides valuable insight into industry sector margin averages, and also allows trend forecasts of the likely impact of value chain power movement. This can be used in conjunction with basic economic supply-demand formula, to look at price and volume elasticity if assumed moves can be made for the competitive make-up of the sector.

Prisoner games

In the 1980s' film, *War Games*, a masterful professor invents a computer that runs the American defence system, controls its nuclear arsenal and has the ability to simulate all forms of war settings in order to develop the most effective counter-strategy. This seemed ideal until the computer decided that playing real war games is far more fun than simulating them, and it begins the process of planning a full nuclear war with Russia which it believes it statistically can win. The world is saved by a smart thinking teenager who loads the child's game, Tic-Tac-Toe, into the computer's memory. The computer quickly realizes that by trying every combination, the game is a zero sum game (i.e. it can never be won) and applies this learning to global war, thus deciding to power down for the rest of eternity because nuclear war is futile.

The second tool is roughly along these lines, although the setting is slightly more realistic and less dramatic. It attempts to model likely reactions from competitors and customers to competitive actions that the collaboration could choose to take, and ensures that those actions do not outweigh the theoretical benefits that can be achieved via the collaboration. A wide

[1] PIMS (Profit Impact of Market Strategy) is a large scale study designed to measure the relationship between business relationships and business results.

range of models can support this, right up to Monte Carlo simulation (i.e. a method for evaluating probability), but at its simplest level, 'war games' is the most commonly used. Executives attempt to put themselves in the shoes of their competitors or customers, imagine owning their resources, and devise possible counter-competitive strikes. This could result in forming alternative competitive collaborations, pricing actions, legal actions, or using existing areas of co-dependency to force back the desired power exchange.

PER (Political Emotional Rational) evaluation

More than any other collaboration model, competitive collaboration is about executives who are prepared to make bold moves that carry potentially steep consequences for themselves and for the corporations they represent. This is particularly challenging where an industry group has maybe 15 executives from different organizations involved. PER evaluation provides a framework to take each one of the individuals and to develop a strategy of engagement for them. It recognizes that to gain agreement, the individual has to be moved along three levels:

1 **Political** – How can this decision form a political win for the organization represented? What can be done to make participation a good political move? What external drivers or lobbying can be applied to assist this?

2 **Emotional** – How can this decision be a personal win for the executive involved? What are the risks to them and how can they be mitigated? What is the personal gain that the individual could achieve through this collaboration and how can that be communicated?

3 **Rational** – What facts show that the collaboration has a clear economic business case? How can that be risk assessed to show that expected returns are positive?

Combining actions in each of these three decision-making zones for all parties involved is a powerful tool to enable ultimate consensus to be gained.

OPERATING MODEL

For the other three models of collaboration, we have considered the five key elements of operating model – location, interfaces, risks, technology and place of belonging. None of these are particularly relevant or indeed appropriate components for the operating model of a competitive collaboration. Risk is probably the sole exception. The operating model for a competitive collaboration is typically through a collaboration board structure, which involves the key players that have put the collaboration together. There will be execution activities, but this will happen almost exclusively in the home organizations. Sometimes, even the marketing and PR (Public Relations) element is not required if the collaboration is one of 'invisible collaboration' from the customer's perspective. This differs if it is an industry-based model, for example, a new trading exchange. However, then the whole entity model from proposition-based collaboration can be applied.

Let's consider risk. This is clearly the process to be monitored, but in a different way to other collaboration models. The major risks are likely to be:

☐ Response from competitors that attempt to negate the impact of the collaboration.

☐ Negative feedback from customers who are concerned if they perceive a shift in power.

☐ Negative PR if the business press publish a story.

☐ 'Non-compliance' by collaborative partners, particularly where success may involve information sharing on specific customers or prospects.

☐ Concern or 'noises' made by a competition authority.

☐ Operational execution issue where one party is not meeting its accountability obligations.

The first key input to the collaboration board meetings is to create a risk register and to agree the appropriate mechanism to collect this data. The second key input is to ensure that the performance of the collaboration can be clearly monitored. This usually involves two sets of measurements – activity measures (e.g. number of leads identified, number of customers contacted), and output measures (e.g. growth in market share, average selling price). Together, the risk register and the performance measures provide the basis for the *modus operandi* of this collaboration model.

Where the collaboration is an industry-based model, the risk of collaboration partner compliance is probably more important. Often, these forms of collaboration are based upon commitments of procurement spend, logistics volume or something similar. Monitoring that each party is meeting its (often contractual) obligation to the collaboration is an additional item.

COMMON PITFALLS

Because of the delicate balance of customer concern, legal constraint and competitor response, competition collaborations are full of pitfalls. The key ones to consider are:

☐ **Assess response** – Never assume that all other factors will remain the same after the collaboration has been put in place. Competitive industries are dynamic and an action by one party will undoubtedly lead to a counter-action elsewhere. Model these potential impacts into the business case.

☐ **Forget trust and partnership** – While these may be a feature, even in a competitive collaboration, the collaboration has to stand up based on the raw economic advantage it gives to both parties. If it does not, it will not succeed.

☐ **Consider competition law** – This exists at two levels. Firstly, at the creation of the collaboration, clear and informed guidance is needed from a legal firm that can guide when the facts are unclear. Secondly, should a negative ruling result regarding the collaboration, the parties must have agreed upfront how it will be handled.

☐ **Focus on the individual** – Although these collaborations are formed corporation-to-corporation, they require bold individuals to make them happen. Gaining consensus often requires a focus on helping individuals to overcome personal risk (whether that be political, emotional or actual) to enable a collaboration to happen.

SUMMARY

1 Competitive collaborations are not about improving cost, quality or service, but about shifting power from one part of the value chain to another.

2 The scope of the collaboration is based generally on organizations bringing either or both a group of customers that are channel managed in some way and a product or service offering, appropriate for that customer set.

3 The basis for the collaboration is economic advantage and this must be quantified and compelling for each party. For a competitive collaboration, softer collaboration benefits cannot replace this.

4 The scope of activities for the participating organizations does not increase, apart from a minor modification if new pricing propositions are used.

5 There are two broad types of competitive collaborations: company-to-company and industry groups, which can involve as many as 20 organizations.

6 The primary focus for contractual issues is on the national or regional competition laws.

7 Individual and corporate risk is high when competitive collaborations go wrong. Using a framework that considers political, emotional and rational reasons can bring executives to the decision-making table and help to facilitate competitive collaborations.

8 Risk needs to be aggressively managed and this requires monitoring legal, competitive, customer and partner actions.

PART 3

OPERATING COLLABORATIVE RELATIONSHIPS

CHAPTER 6

COLLABORATION ESTABLISHMENT

FOLLOW THE PROCESS

Chapters 2–5 considered each of the four models of strategic collaboration – supply chain, capability-based, proposition-based and competitive collaboration. We now know *what* type of models can and should be used, but not *how* to go about establishing the collaboration. What process can an organization go through to put any of these models in place? What are the tools, templates and checklists that can be used along the way? What are the pitfalls and the lessons learned?

Collaboration establishment is essentially a change management process – like so many that organizations will have run within their own corporate boundaries. And as such it needs the same starting point; a clear route map which can ensure its success.

Although the four models each exist to support a different type of collaboration goal that has different business drivers, scope, risk profile and focuses, the broad process steps by which these are established are similar and fall into five main phases:

1 **Evaluating business case** – Setting in place a clear and compelling rationale for the creation of the collaboration as an entity and for each of the participating organizations at the beginning.

2 **Transformation design and planning** – Designing the shape and structure of the collaboration and being explicit on the performance outputs that it is able to achieve.

3 **Joint implementation planning** – Conducting the detailed design in terms of people, processes and relationship, which will form the *modus operandi* of the collaboration.

4 **Implementation** – Executing the agreed plan using a cross-company model, which ensures that the design aspirations are translated into operating reality.

5 **Evaluating results** – Creating an ongoing mechanism for 'business as usual' operations of the collaboration, and creating the review and evaluation of the collaboration's performance.

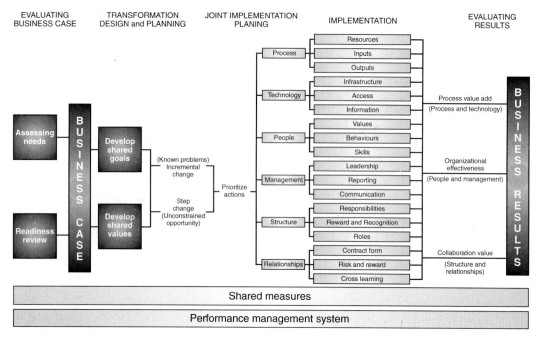

FIGURE 6.1: Collaboration establishment framework

It is critical that collaboration establishment is seen as a single integrated process. By following these steps, common problems can be avoided and a complete approach taken. Because each of the four collaboration models are different from each other in almost all aspects, the way in which each step may be applied will be slightly different in each situation, and certainly the output of that step (the *what*) will be unique – however the process itself remains consistent.

EVALUATING BUSINESS CASE

Before setting off on the collaboration journey, each potential participant needs to critically ask and answer two questions:

1 Why am I doing this?

2 Am I ready to do this, and do I think they are?

The first step that any organization must undertake to answer question one is a review and deployment of their own strategy. Business strategies take many forms, but it is most useful in this instance to convert the strategy into a set of simple goal-oriented statements. This could include: 'We wish to grow market share in segment X by 10 per cent', 'We wish new products to account for 25 per cent of our revenue' or 'We want our service staff to be upper quartile in both experience and pay for this industry'. Thus, we have a baseline position for the strategic goal of the organization.

Against each statement a column can be created called 'Collaboration contribution'. Identify within the column if a proposed collaboration could add value, and to which of the strategic statements. Once this process has been completed two things become apparent:

1 How the collaboration can or cannot contribute to the strategic objectives of the organization.

2 Which collaboration model is appropriate.

If there are no areas where the proposed collaboration will make a material impact to a strategic goal, then either our list of strategic statements is incomplete, or this is not a candidate for a collaboration approach. An alternative relationship model may be more suitable. The type of statements that the collaboration support also indicate the right model for collaboration – supply chain, capability-based, proposition-based or competitive. The statements can also highlight where there could be goal confusion, for example if we are looking for a single collaboration to meet a very broad range of strategic goals.

Strategic fit is understood, but not strategic contribution. To what degree can the collaboration help to meet our strategic goals? Will it deliver 1 per cent of them, 10 per cent or 100 per cent? For each of the goals identified as potentially supported by the collaboration, there is a second process that identifies how large a contribution the collaboration could make to each goal. This can be done by looking at a one, three and five-year time horizon and asking the question: 'If the collaboration was successful, what percentage of this strategic goal would it achieve?'

Once this final step is completed, we are in a position to produce a statement of strategic need. This clearly articulates which of our own organization's strategic goals the collaboration could support, to what degree it could support them and gives a first assessment of the quantification of this (i.e. how the collaboration could impact the strategic measures). It also identifies which form of collaboration model is appropriate and provides one other insight – a first perspective on likely risk at both a corporate and collaboration level. At the corporate level, the statement reports how much reliance we plan to put on this particular collaboration in terms of meeting the strategic goals, and at the collaboration level due to the model this entails, what level of upside and downside risk we should plan for.

We now know what the business need for this collaboration is, but do we know if we are ready? Is there the right cultural environment to make a collaboration work? Do we and our prospective partners have a compatibility of style? Do our values align or oppose? As Professor Richard Lamming of Bath Business School notes, 'poor foundations and divergent goals have been the cause of most alliance failures'. We need to understand our readiness.

Readiness review

To know whether organizations can work together, the organizations need to understand themselves first. Specifically this addresses three areas:

1 What are the prevailing cultural norms?

2 What is the 'rewarded' management style?

3 What is the normal operating model, in terms of decision making, performance management and risk appetite?

Answering these questions requires a readiness assessment to be carried out, normally through focus groups or focus interviews. This uses a structured set of questions based around each of these areas. It is critically important that each of the potential collaborative partners agree to conduct the same assessment process. In this way, when the process moves into joint planning, there is a common basis for discussion around cultural alignment and the creation of a new and common model of operating. It is often easier to plot the outcome from this assessment on a spider diagram, so that areas of similarity and difference between the prospective parties are made apparent.

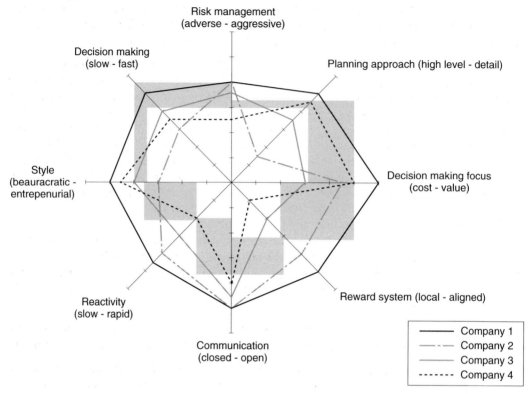

FIGURE 6.2: Example readiness assessment output

TRANSFORMATION DESIGN AND PLANNING

The starting point for transformation design and planning should be that each participating organization has completed its own readiness assessment and has its own statement of strategic need. The organization should have its own clarity about why it is sitting at the collaboration table, what it hopes to achieve, and what sort of cultural environment it is coming from. The challenge is to go through a process that takes those sets of individual needs and seeks to understand whether there is a common basis for moving forward.

Sharing the statements of strategic need, or more specifically each party presenting to one another their expectations of what the collaboration could achieve, begins the process of building a strategic vision for the collaboration itself. This is where the process of alignment really starts. Drawing from the set of strategic needs statements, can a new document be produced that contains a sufficient percentage of each party's hopes for making the collaboration a reality? Where compromise is needed or where individual company goals are divergent, can common ground be found that is equal to all parties, or does one organization have to give back far more than the others?

Facilitated workshops can be used to develop a set of strategic goals for the collaboration, and again these are most useful if they are based upon a set of strategic objectives statements and supporting measures. This makes expectations tangible and understandable. If it is a supply chain collaboration, this may be based around delivered unit cost or fulfilment rate, if a capability-based collaboration, it may be number of patents achieved and new product success rate, if a proposition-based collaboration, it could be market share and gross margin, and for a competitive collaboration, cross-sell ratio and penetration rate.

Once the set of collaboration strategic goals is defined, there is real value in going back and testing both individual company goal fulfilment and true alignment. In other words, take the collaboration strategic goals and map them back to each of the individual statements of strategic need to see what percentage of their desired position has been met, and whether this is roughly consistent. In the enthusiasm to get a collaboration going, organizations sometimes overlook whether they have developed a compromise solution that provides real strategic value back into each organization – this is particularly critical for competitive collaborations. It is far better to force that issue early, rather than after investments have been made and positions taken. Now we know what we want to achieve, but can we work together?

Cultural alignment

In Chapters 2–5 we saw that the need for cultural fit between collaboration organizations varies depending on the model of collaboration used. It even varies within each model. However, even in competitive collaboration, understanding some of the key cultural elements that relate to decision making and risk appetite are helpful when considering if the collaboration is likely to succeed.

Chapter 8 covers how to make cultural alignment happen in an operational sense in detail, but at this stage in the collaboration establishment process it is important to do three things:

1 Develop and document a set of statements that define the cultural and values norms of the collaboration, in a manner appropriate to the collaboration model used (see Chapter 8).

2 Identify the gap for each organization between their assessment output and the desired collaboration approach.

3 Consider the implications on success if organizations operate in their 'parent' model rather than in the agreed collaboration style.

JOINT IMPLEMENTATION PLANNING

We know what the collaboration wishes to achieve, but not how it will make that a reality. Implementation planning turns high-level design ideas into the detailed delivery model for the collaboration. For the whole entity option this is a substantive exercise, for others less so. The first step is to understand how radical we need to be if the agreed collaboration goals are going to be met.

Let us take the example of a supply chain collaboration in the oil industry. Imagine that a platform operator and a well-drilling contractor choose to create a collaboration that has, as its stated goal, cutting the cost of well development by 30 per cent, with the key measure being cost per metre of well sunk. Through the collaboration, we have for the first time the collective resources, information and design knowledge of both organizations sitting in the same room, working together to achieve this aim.

The problem can be tackled by considering first all of the current issues associated with this process. For example,

☐ The companies inspect one another's work.

☐ The information which would be useful to one party is kept confidential.

☐ The commercial contract makes cost reduction an unattractive goal for the contractor.

☐ The contractor risk in their supply market, that they factor into the pricing schedule.

☐ The known error and re-work loops due to poor planning.

Each of these areas can be identified, evaluated and solutions developed for them. These are the known opportunities – the areas that can be most readily identified and remedied. Once this part of the planning process is complete, the areas can be summarized and their impact on the key measure – cost per metre – evaluated. Then comes the key question: 'Will this enable the collaboration to achieve its target?' If it does, great, but if not then a more radical approach is needed. This will consider the unconstrained opportunities.

Returning to our well-drilling collaboration. If the known opportunities were all fully addressed, this only gives a 12 per cent reduction. Where is the other 18 per cent to come from? Some 'out of the box' thinking is needed. By this process of thinking through the more radical solutions to the collaborations goals, the design of the collaboration itself is formed. Perhaps we find that a significant portion of cost is due to the travel costs of the contractor drilling crews; the oil platform operator could make space to locate them offshore on the rig to solve this. Perhaps both firms are using seismic equipment to the same end and the collaboration recognizes that both parties do not need to lease this; cost can be removed if that asset is shared. Maybe there is a new engineering design that the collective engineering capability of the two organizations could put into operation.

Together, this list of known improvements and unconstrained opportunities describes the plan for the collaboration, and from it the design of structure, roles, processes and information technology needs will simply fall into place. Two other elements, however, are critical at this point:

1 The measurement model, which forms the basis for collaboration review and management, needs to be completed and built before moving into implementation. This is the common and shared data which is available to all parties, forms the basis for reporting, informs decision making and makes strategic alignment an operational reality. Even within single organizations it is common to see different managers reporting the same metrics in different ways. Collaborations cannot afford this confusion.

2 Now is the time to establish contractual arrangements between the parties, or indeed for the new entity creation if that is the chosen model. Only at the point when implementation planning is complete and it is known at an operational level how this collaboration will work, where it will be located and who does what, can the contracts and commercials be completed. This is a challenge, because organizations will already have committed resource, taken risks, shared competitively sensitive information and so forth. The simplest parallel is to consider the phase until this point in the same manner as organizations who consider merging. They operate for a period under a Heads of Agreement model which covers the confidentiality, commercial risk and also outlines how costs are shared if the collaboration does not proceed (this normally involves each party paying for their own costs).

IMPLEMENTATION

The design can now be put into operational reality. The most important success factor to ensure that implementation goes smoothly is to have completed a well thought out implementation planning process. Assuming that has happened, what key things can make the difference at this point? Phasing strategy is important – which bits to implement when?

The implementation of a collaboration strategy is no different to any other implementation process. There are stakeholders who observe the process. Some are supportive; others will be resistant. It is important that demonstrable proof that the collaboration goals and process can deliver the overall aims is given early. Quick wins within the implementation process are critical to support this need. We also know, from the assessment process, where the cross-company cultural challenges lie, and where those could derail the process or at least 'sparks could fly' when implementation really digs in. Move these either upfront, to get through them quickly, or raise them later when the momentum generated by the quick wins will help to push them through more rapidly. Timing is key for implementation. In addition, there are other guiding principles that can be applied to the implementation phase. We will focus on seven:

1 **Establish implementation monitoring** – This needs to consider two elements: activity achievement (are we hitting milestones?) and output success (did those milestones deliver the results we expected?).

2 **Put in appropriate governance** – Implementation is a different operating model to 'business as usual'. The governance model designed for the collaboration may not be the right one for this initial start-up phase.

3 **Focus on locations and roles** – Design documents often tend to be too conceptual. Implementation happens at the places where people work and it addresses their roles. Use job roles at the point of implementation as the 'common currency' for driving through implementation.

4 **Keep short accounts** – During implementation, the cultural integration challenges most readily show themselves because this is a period of uncertainty. Have a daily process for raising this and resolving issues – do not allow these issues to grow.

5 **Deliver the enablers early** – We have already talked about the measurement model, but there are other key enablers that help to provide a sound foundation. This may be the physical location, the technology infrastructure or personal employment contracts. Omitting these until later can be an enormous distraction to the staff involved.

6 **Aggressively manage risk** – Establish a single risk process that explicitly identifies, for each risk, who will bear the main pain if that risk happens (by collaboration partner). This helps to engender a common understanding of each organization's positions through implementation, as well as the information from which risks can be managed away.

7 **Have a formal sign-off process** – The danger with implementation is that it is not seen as a phase in its own right. Implementation evolves into 'business as usual'. There should be an end of phase checklist and, once each element of the design is in place and confirmed through completing the checklist, it should be signed off by the collaboration board, ready for ongoing operation.

EVALUATING RESULTS

Ongoing management is where the governance model designed at the start plays its full role. Assuming that the roles and responsibilities of this governance structure have been outlined clearly (using RACI), there are two things to focus on at this final phase:

1 What information does the collaboration board and other key governance groups review?

2 How do they review the information and drive improvement?

The answer to the first question is relatively straightforward. The measures model drives the meeting agenda. But what about performance management? The heart of that process needs to be a closed loop plan-do-review process, which will have four key components:

1 A review of the results of performance, based on the output from the measures model appropriate to that governance group.

2 An evaluation of root cause of areas that are either significantly exceeding performance targets, or any areas that are falling short. In a collaboration that has multiple levels in the governance, it is important that the review process happens at the lowest level first and then feeds up, so that when the collaboration board is reviewing performance, those at the meetings will be informed from lower level meetings around potential root cause.

3 Agreement to the actions necessary to close the performance gap and a clear allocation of both the accountability and the time frame to do it.

4 An evaluation of the effectiveness of the improvement actions, both in terms of whether they have been executed and more importantly, whether the assumed relationship identified during the root cause step, between that action and its impact on the appropriate performance measure, has happened. If it has not, then the root cause exercise needs to be repeated to identify what other actions must be taken.

This fourth and final step in the performance management process is the most critical to ensure that collaboration goals are met, and it is the step most commonly left out. The review process is not only about following these steps, there are three key behaviours that are fundamental to its success:

1 Under-performing areas or processes previously 'hidden', are quickly exposed, forcing managers to take **accountability** for their performance.

2 Executives, managers and supervisors who lead performance review meetings must **challenge** poor performance and seek out root causes.

3 Corrective actions agreed must be planned on a timely basis. People are thus forced to take accountability for **delivering results** if the review process is to add any value.

The output of this performance review not only drives the day-to-day management of the collaboration, but also informs the integrated planning process as the shape, focus and deliverables of the collaboration evolve over time.

CRITICAL SUCCESS FACTORS

There are many critical success factors for a collaboration to be effectively established, but there are four factors that reviews of successful and failed collaborations routinely show to be important when separating the winners from the losers. Chapters 7–10 focus on these four critical areas and provide detailed examples, templates and practical application. These four factors are:

1 **Partner selection** – Choosing the right organizations to embark on this collaboration journey with. Often organizations take this route with firms they have a historic relationship with, believing this will make it more likely to succeed. Often the reverse actually happens, because a full establishment process is not followed, and also because the fact that an existing relationship does not necessarily mean that the organization is the best partner available.

2 **Common goals and values** – In this chapter we have discussed the mechanism for producing a statement of goals and values. The critical challenge, however, is to operate a collaboration that has common goals and values. These are two very different issues and the method to achieve the latter is the priority.

3 **Integrated planning** – Within an organization, integrated planning is the process by which individual functions or business units are aligned behind the corporate goals. Within a collaboration this process is even more important because multiple organizations are involved.

4 **Measurement** – The creation of a single, common and consistent measurement model is the underpinning tool around which success is monitored, performance gaps closed and decisions made. It is the foundation for the collaboration.

SUMMARY

1 The four collaboration models define *what* the collaboration should look like, the collaboration establishment process describes *how* that model can be executed.

2 Collaboration establishment is similar to any change process, requiring a clear routemap.

3 A common collaboration establishment process can be used for all four models, recognizing that the outcome of the process will be very different for each.

4 The establishment process has five key steps: evaluating the business case, transformation design and planning, joint implementation planning, implementation and evaluating results.

5 During business case evaluating, the two critical steps are to undertake a needs assessment for each participating organization, and a readiness review which considers the cultural environment and values.

6 Transformation design takes these two inputs and, through a facilitated process, develops a common set of goals and values for the collaboration.

7 Implementation planning defines how those goals will be achieved on a day-to-day operating basis, and considers both known improvements and unconstrained opportunities. From this combined list, the structure, governance, processes and commercial model logically fall.

8 Implementation is where the real work gets done and is assisted by a clear phasing strategy that delivers early wins, applying the seven guiding principles for implementation delivery. The most important principle is to formally sign off the end of implementation so that there is a shift into 'business as usual', not an evolution.

9 Evaluating results is dependent upon all parties creating and using the measures model, and also upon a four-step performance management process which looks at performance, identifies root cause reasons for gaps, agrees and allocates actions, and then monitors action completion and its effectiveness against the key performance measures.

CHAPTER 7

PARTNER SELECTION

IT'S NOT ABOUT WHO YOU KNOW

How do the vast majority of partners that work together in a collaboration find out about each other? Normally they have already been trading together, but in a different form of relationship. In other words, most collaborations involve organizations who already know one another, and who make an opportunistic decision to pursue a collaboration route that could lead to improved performance for both parties. This is not the intended purpose or the starting point for collaborative relationships. We have already shown that a collaborative relationship is, by definition, one that is strategic. If it is strategic, then the starting point is recognition of a strategic gap – whether of capability, performance or market dominance or access – and evaluating potential options to close that gap. Options include organically filling it, a merger or acquisition, a joint venture of some description or a collaborative arrangement. Collaboration, therefore, is only one of a number of potential options, and whether it is appropriate is about what you need, not about whom you know.

Let us assume that the gap analysis against the strategy has taken place. There are three or four identified gaps where a collaboration is seen to be an appropriate solution – what happens now? Do you canvass the room to find out who knows some companies that might fit the bill? Do you print out the supplier list and consider the companies with which you seem to get along with well? Of course not. For many companies, choosing a collaboration partner is a decision that lasts ten to 15 years. In private life, you would not choose a partner by asking your colleagues for ideas and then picking one. And this is how it should be within the corporate sphere. What is needed is an analytical and rigorous approach to selecting candidates for that critical relationship.

A structured approach

Choosing potential partners to participate in a collaboration effort is about managing a 'funnel'. At one end of the funnel all potential partners should be considered; being broad on criteria may help to contemplate more radical collaboration solutions. However, that long list of potential candidates needs to be narrowed quickly to a very short-list of real prospects, before the major effort of face-to-face interactions is expended. For each of the four models of collaboration the funnel's criteria will be substantially different, and so will be the point when potential partners should be contacted. Nevertheless, the overall process itself will be, in principal, the same.

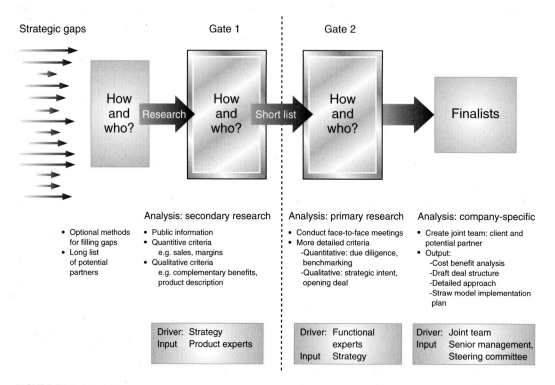

FIGURE 7.1: Partner selection process

An effective partner selection process, as outlined in Figure 7.1, is characterized by a number of factors.

☐ **Strategically driven** – The only input to the process is the identified gaps from the strategy. It does not use short-term operational pressures, or immediate market needs. Instead, the length and importance of such a relationship model is driven by the only item a business has which matches that level of priority and longevity – the business strategy.

☐ **Objective** – In most partner selection processes, personal agenda at an executive level come into play and, once the process is visible, influence will be exerted by the potential partner community. That is why the process needs to be laid out at the beginning and to be clearly auditable.

☐ **Criteria-based** – Not only do criteria support the principle of objectivity, they also force a discipline to ensure that your organization's aims are clear from the outset, and that strategic fit is commonly understood.

☐ **Resource appropriate** – Partner selection warrants sufficient senior level resource to manage the process effectively. However, the selection process should be designed such that this resource effort is applied towards a small group of highly likely collaborative partners, not against a broad base of 'half chances'. This is why a step gating mechanism is critical, where measures track the process at certain points.

☐ **Multi-stepped** – This is where the gates come into their own. The model we have shown in Figure 7.1 can be applied to most situations. However, sometimes more gates, even up to four are needed. The priority is to put a gate into the process at each point where additional information gained through resource effort allows a material percentage of firms still on the list to be exited. This allows both the principles of criteria-based and resource appropriate to be met.

☐ **Data-driven** – The only way for a process to be robust is if each step is data-driven. For some elements of evaluation, like financial performance, this is evident and easy to do. Others, such as cultural fit, capability or customer satisfaction are less obvious. It is important, however, that a quantitative process is devised – even if, in the end, it is a subjective score out of ten by the evaluation team, with reasons for that score. This gives clarity, forces objectivity and supports decision making.

Agreeing the selection process is an important stand-alone activity in its own right. Start this from the above set of design intents. Once the design intents are agreed by the key executive group, the process can be confirmed. In essence, this is about defining the gating points, what criteria there will be at each point, what sources of information will be used within each step between two gates, who will be involved in collecting that information, and who will decide ultimately which companies get through a gate.

There are other considerations throughout this process. When and how should a commercial conversation begin with potential partners? It is naïve to believe that this cannot happen during the process, although it is desirable that commercial and fit processes happen separately. Will this be a process which is visible to the marketplace, and if so when? The answer to this question is often model-driven. Usually, competitive collaborations do not wish to have any market communication, and certainly not during the selection process. Others, particularly capability-based collaborations benefit from such visibility. And finally, how many organizations do we expect to carry through at each gate? In part, this is determined by appropriate resource effort, and in part by the view of the additional benefits this process can bring to the organization (i.e. from the discussions which happen with key players in the industry value chain as a result of the process). It is not uncommon to identify different views on how collaborations could happen and what scope they could take once the two-way debate occurs.

The crucial deliverable upfront, is that the agreed decision-making executive group have collectively signed off and authorized the process to be used. This process must reflect the design intents agreed, and can be used as the point of reference if potential disagreements emerge about the right collaborative partners to use.

BUILDING THE LONG LIST

We have agreed a process. To kick-start the process, a long list of companies needs to be built. How is that done? With the rapid consolidation taking place within industries and the convergence of industry players, it is no longer always obvious where to seek out an appropriate collaboration partner. It is not just about who can do what today – it is about strategic intent. In what direction are these organizations going within the time frame of the collaborative relationship? Are Wal-Mart or Tesco only food retailers? Certainly not. Are the major telephone operators communications companies, infrastructure companies or media companies? Has content overtaken the medium through which it is delivered? And what of the old construction companies, are they in the business of building things, or are they facilities management (FM) firms who deliver fully-maintained locations? All relevant questions with one simple conclusion. The boundaries that define industry focus – vertical boundaries or core capabilities – are blurring at an increasing rate and the implication for the long list is to think widely and be unconstrained.

Where to look?

In order to build that effective long list, some basic demographic criteria is required. Fortunately, all registered companies in most developed nations have government-run registration mechanisms, such as Companies House in the UK. These mechanisms provide the data source to match criteria to real organizations. Similarly, commercial firms in the US like Dun and Bradstreet, Fortune or Standard and Poor provide a similar offering. The list needs to be broad and so the demographic criteria, at this stage, can be relatively simple. They will typically contain some or all of the following factors:

☐ **Company size** – What is the minimum or maximum turnover level appropriate to the type of collaboration being considered?

☐ **Geographical presence** – Are there specific markets the partner must operate in, or indeed areas where they should be absent?

☐ **Industry focus** – In which industry sector should the firm be based, or is that irrelevant?

☐ **Financial stability** – Is a basic financial strength needed from a prospective partner, perhaps indicated by either credit rating, gearing (level of debt as a percentage of total capital) or profit growth?

☐ **Length of trading** – Is it important for the potential partner to have a reasonable trading record?

Supply chain and capability-based collaborations are the two most challenging collaboration models to build the long list for. Consider the example of a food manufacturer who produces both fresh and frozen foods. Following a review of their strategy, they recognize that to operate a supply chain network which uses multi-compartmented vehicles and has state of the art distribution centres, appropriate to the key supermarket customers, requires a capability they are more likely to find through a collaborative relationship, rather than building it in-house. The question, therefore, is where to find a partner with this capability? Evidently the third-party logistics organizations would be on the list, but other sources could ultimately prove richer pickings. The supermarkets may wish to move one step back up the value chain, and so they can go on the list. Other food manufacturers must deal with the same issue, and perhaps one would see this as an opportunity to share logistics costs and to build a world-class infrastructure. What about national food chains? They must send delivery trucks with both ambient and refrigerated compartments up and down the high street every day. Could they be a candidate? Perhaps the petrol filling stations who have expanded their retail supply chain capability will be potentially suitable. Alternatively, do any of these candidates have a collaborative arrangement which could be joined, rather than setting one up from scratch?

The obvious list of third-party logistics providers can suddenly grow into a whole host of other organizations. Identifying these firms is often more challenging in the case of supply chain collaborations or capability-based collaborations, because they tend to be more internally oriented. If you have designed a new value proposition and you know what a partner needs to bring because that is their marketplace offering, it is visible and easy to identify. Similarly, competitive collaboration is solely concerned with channels to market and customer base – all very much in the public domain.

With supply chain and capability-based collaboration models, more time should be allowed to build up the list. Brainstorm all types of possible organizations, search the databases and involve the third-party organizations that operate in this area. Once we have that long list, the process is ready to start. We have got 200 prospects – which is the one?

GATE 1 – SECONDARY RESEARCH

The general principle for the first gate (see Figure 7.1) is that its criteria should all be available through secondary data sources. If, at this first decision-making step, direct engagement with prospective organizations is needed, then the resource effort grows exponentially. There is a risk of embarrassment if an organization is approached this early in the process, before the criteria for a collaborative partner is known.

Given that at this step only secondary information sources can be used, considerations are limited. However, for most medium and large organizations, it is surprising what can be gathered from annual accounts, press releases, online news reporting systems and so on. The following 12 key criteria outline the most common areas to consider at this point.

1 Strategic fit

Overall vision and mission of the organization. Key statements of strategic intent, which can normally be found in press releases (often when financial results are declared) or at the front of the financial statements. Company websites can help enormously to provide this information. Other useful data sources are both the industry and financial analysts who monitor the sector – they will provide a critique of the stated strategic direction. These strategic statements, from the various sources, can be summarized and contrasted to the statement of strategic need, which was developed to provide a score for apparent fit. At this point it will be relatively subjective, but supported by factual information.

2 Differentiation strategy

The information, which provides data on strategic fit, will also typically include comments about how the organization attempts to differentiate its customers. This will relate to one of three areas: lowest price, best product/service or market differentiated. Where press releases exist relating to new customer 'wins', these may contain some of the reasons why that firm was chosen by its customer and provide further insight.

3 Geographical footprint

The registered accounts in most countries require organizations to split out their revenues and profits by geographical area. This document will also commonly contain a list of all subsidiary organizations operated around the world, as well as any franchise, dealer or value-added reseller (VAR) contracts. It is important to try and understand where the firm is trading, what volume of sales comes from each region, and how the organization appears to be growing or shrinking its footprint.

4 Product and service offering

Unlike understanding differentiation, which is a more strategic evaluation, this criterion attempts to appreciate the simple facts of how many SKUs the organization has, whether they are grouped into product or service ranges, and what statements have been made about where that product or service range is going. In addition to some of the sources already mentioned, most firms have a PR function from which product information can be obtained. Registrations with trademark or patent bodies are useful, in particular those which are pending give an indication of future direction. Often the organization structure itself, which for many firms is published on their website, may be designed around the key product and service areas.

5 Customer scope

Firstly, consider the base data. Does the company declare how many customers it has, and if so are they categorized in some manner, either by geography or by segment? The organization structure itself may be modelled around customer groupings. The key information to obtain is where the organization focuses its efforts and, therefore, which customer groups it either specifically tries to retain, or more commonly acquire. Basic marketing information from the organization, the key messages it puts out through PR or on its website, will often provide insight into this area.

6 Financial structure

How is the business financed? Critical measures to consider are the debt versus equity splits. Is the equity commonly traded, privately held, or a mixture? What level of equity is held by active board members? Are there significant options set against the firm's equity base and who owns what? Are there major institutional shareholders and have they made any statements about their holdings? Financial structure also needs to consider where debt comes from and what level of preference is given to that debt. Moving below the parent firm, what subsidiary or partial ownerships exist and what level of consolidation feeds back into the holding structure?

7 Customer satisfaction

Often more difficult to collect, but there is a growing body of third-party market and customer information. Is the organization an industry, like utilities or telecommunications, where there may be a government complaints agency? Have any of the fair trading organizations received complaints? Is the company covered by one of the major market research firms, and has this coverage included a customer perspective? Other financial indicators can also give a view towards customer satisfaction. Perhaps revenue per customer, churn rates or stock return or rejects.

8 Employee commitment

This is undoubtedly the hardest area of all to gain useful and quantified information at this point. However, there are still some places to look. Sometimes firms share attrition rates, others break out recruitment costs, which are good indicators of non-growth related turnover. In addition, there are an increasing number of external surveys ranging from graduate views on who are the best employers, through to workforce motivation studies that rank the bigger and better known firms.

9 Revenue growth

Drawn directly from published accounts, the key aspects to look at are three to five year trends. Be careful to split out items such as discontinued operations, changes to accounting policy (if they have taken place during that period), the impact of any acquisitions or divestments, and if relevant, account for currency fluctuations. Although history is helpful, the future is more important. The firm will undoubtedly have declared its own view, but the industry and market analysts will add useful perspective.

10 Profit performance

Like revenue, the accounts can provide the base data. Apply the same rules for acquisitions, divestments, accounting changes, discontinued operations and so forth. However, the additional factor for profit is to decide which definition is most useful. Is it the trading performance, the bottom line number, or higher up the profit and loss (P&L) statement, focusing more on product and service margin? The analysts and the company will have a view about the future trends, which can overlay historical fact.

11 Cost and cash management

This is a simple case of examining the trends of each of the relevant lines in the published accounts, typically using a three to five year time horizon. Often there is little to inform about the future performance of key cost elements, so statistical trends are a good second substitute. Applying simple ratios, such as payroll/revenue, stock/sales days, working capital/shareholders funds, can bring additional insight.

12 Business stability

This final review area attempts to identify a potential discontinuity that could make historical performance trends irrelevant. Is a big lawsuit coming along? Do critical patents run out soon? What do the credit agencies offer and has that changed? Is the cash position solid versus future commitments? Is the revenue profile from strong historic customer relationships or is it fluid? Does the balance sheet contain real assets or mostly goodwill?

There may be 100 or more organizations on the long list for which this information is being collected. Therefore, it is helpful to be explicit about how 'automated' this first screen is. Specifically, if for each firm there are 20 quantified pieces of data collected and there are 150 firms involved, that is 3000 facts around which to make a decision. Do they each carry equal weight? Are some of them 'must haves' while others are 'nice to haves'? Are some of them yes/no considerations, and others on an improving scale?

In most instances a weighted scoring scheme is developed initially and, as the information is collected, an overall evaluation for each company evolves. This enables objectivity, but can be treated with flexibility. If, as real data is collected, it is apparent that some of the weightings are inappropriate, the model can be easily amended.

First thoughts on collaboration design

Having compiled the full list of prospective partner information, the concept of the collaboration begins to take shape. This is a useful point to consider what this collaboration could look like. Is it a two-company affair, or will multiple partners provide the best solution? Is one type of solution emerging from the data, or could two or three different options meet the strategic need? Do prospective partners look like competitors, existing suppliers or customers? What is the best way to approach them? How should the commercial discussion be broached? Is there a risk to existing relationships when the approach is made? What are the downside risks if we engage with a prospective partner and subsquently do not choose them? Could there be a negative response? The answers to these questions are not needed this early in the process, but it is a useful time to sketch out four:

1 A document that outlines collaboration options and their respective pros and cons.

2 A view on the expected number of organizations in the collaboration.

3 A risk register, which at this point will focus particularly on customers, suppliers and competitors.

4 An issues log, which captures all of the questions raised, and with it a decision log. At this stage in the process, decisions are often impossible and, therefore, the use of 'working assumptions' is helpful. Essentially, these form the basis by which the process is managed, going forward. They are the *de facto* decision, until more information becomes available to prove them wrong, or until enough is known and they can be confirmed as a definite decision and moved onto the decision log.

GATE 2 – PRIMARY RESEARCH

Depending on the complexity of the selection process, there may be more than one gate before reaching this, the last phase in the process. The number of organizations left in the process, once this final screen is reached, is very important because this is where contact with prospective partners begins. As a general rule of thumb, there should be between two and four times the number of expected parties in the collaboration left in the process. Therefore, if we are expecting to find two organizations for the collaboration, it is appropriate to have between four and eight organizations left in the process at this stage.

Frequently the problem is not reducing the list, but finding enough potential partners. This is why making the long list truly long is such an important success criterion. If this is the case, at least everything that can be done has been done to generate the best possible final list.

Getting ready

To conduct this final screening step, the prospective partner is engaged with directly. Critical precursors to specificy include: the way that confidentiality will be managed, both in terms of information shared and regarding the process itself; and having a clear set of messages which define expectation for the process. What happens if the partner wants to be in a collaboration but they are not selected? What if costs are incurred and the other party walks away? For each prospective partner a 'sales pack' needs to be produced, broadly the same for all prospects, but allowing for specific tailoring. This pack will include the business environment, the factors that led your organization to consider a collaboration, what that would entail and some initial thoughts on its goals and focus. Finally, the initial thinking regarding how commercial and contractual issues will be addressed, needs to be made more tangible. What exactly can we say to the partners at this point about money?

We know how to start the process and have a coherent position on the sales messages, confidentiality agreements and commercial and contractual positions. What additional information should we attempt to collect to carry out the final screening process?

☐ More specific information under the areas of the 12 key criteria used earlier in the process. Examples of the additional facts that direct contact allows could include:

1 **Strategic fit:** Focus Interviews with Executives (the 'reality' behind the official statements); ranked priorities, Executive alignment around goals.

2 **Differentiation strategy:** Feedback from sales and marketing key managers; customer feedback or market research conducted by the firm; review of win/loss reports.

3 **Geographical footprint:** Market expansion plans; plans to change channel structures (such as acquisition of resellers); planned investments.

4 **Product and service offering:** Actual revenues and profits by offering; key items in the new product development pipeline; internal perception of key trademarks or patents; product enhancement plans.

5 **Customer scope:** Segmentation plan; understanding of differentiation of offer across customer groups, also including pricing and discounting schemes; planned and actual growth rates by segment.

6 **Financial structure:** Comparison between management accounts and financial accounts; existance of items not visible through published accounts, such as off-balance sheet finance, pension fund liabilities and so on.

7 **Customer satisfaction:** Value and number of credit notes; a review of customer complaints; evaluation of product returns or replacements; customer satisfaction surveys.

8 **Employee commitments:** Recruitment cycles; staff turnover rates (split by planned and unplanned); internal staff surveys; achievement of training and development goals.

9 **Revenue growth:** Linkage of revenue growth to product and service offering, new product development, and also customer segments.

10 **Profit performance:** Understanding of the actions that have delivered profit growth (revenue focus or cost focus); sustainability of profit contributors; linkage to product/service and customer groups.

11 **Cost and cash management:** Visibility and effectiveness of stock control and credit control; variation of working capital performance between locations, product/service lines and customer segments. Linkage between these areas and growth rates.

12 **Business stability:** Attrition rate amongst top 30 staff; areas of reliance on a few key players; existence and execution of succession planning.

☐ Specific data about the fit of the company with regards to the collaboration goals. This will be model specific, but there are four areas commonly applied: similar values, common maturity, mutuality of benefit and style compatibility.

1 Similar values

At a corporate level (note this may not be needed within the collaboration itself) is there a preparedness to be open about information, to operate in an honest and integral manner? Can trust be built at this executive level? Is there a similar mind-set about improvement and collaboration goal stretch? Does the organization apply a similar decision-making balance across the key stakeholders of shareholder, employee, partner and customer?

2 Common maturity

Is the organization at a similar level in terms of collaboration experience? Is the management approach suitable for operating such processes? Are the necessary skills and competencies in place to enable it to succeed? Is there a similar problem-solving mentality? Does a joint planning culture exist to allow for mature, informed debate across the organizational boundary?

3 Mutuality of benefit

Does the other party see a strategic fit? Does their assessment of strategic need match your own organization? Is there a similar appetite for risk, and does that risk profile reflect the benefits on offer? Is the desire to achieve the potential gain equally strong, and is there an apparent equality about both achieving it and sharing in it?

4 Style compatibility

How similar are the governance models between the businesses? Is authority and responsibility deployed to roughly similar levels, or is one control-oriented and the other empowerment-focused? What is the predominant management philosophy; is it dictatorial or coaching based? What focus is given to staff development and ownership?

As with gate 1, a weighted assessment tool can be used here. This time the scoring should be clearly informed by data, observation and a much softer element based on meeting the people that you would need to work with, if the collaboration is going to be successful.

SHORT-LIST EVALUATION

In the same way that the long list needs to be long, so the short-list must be short. To be specific, it contains only the preferred choice. If it is a one-to-one collaboration, then there is one name on the short-list; the company you most wish to proceed with. If, in the process, others were identified with whom it was felt that a collaboration could work, do not inform them yet of the short-list decision. If the collaboration cannot be made to work with the preferred partner, a new short-list will be needed and can include the other suitable companies. It is also acceptable if there is no name on the short-list. This will be a hard decision at this point, and one that not enough companies make. Although you want to find a way forward, it is best to recognize if one does not exist.

Assume this is a one-to-one collaboration and we have found a preferred partner – what happens now? The collaboration establishment process proper starts. Both parties need to conduct their readiness review and needs assessment to produce their statement of strategic need. For this process to start, an initial contractual arrangement needs to be put in place to replace what was used during the selection process. Normally, at the end of the evaluating the business case phase, a clear decision is required from the boards of the relevant organizations on whether it is a formal choice to proceed to collaboration. After this point there are always exit clauses, but it is now assumed that the collaboration will form unless there is a compelling reason to stop. Until now there has been no assumed outcome.

SUMMARY

1 Only begin the process of collaboration based on an identified strategic gap – never progress for opportunistic or operational convenience reasons.

2 Begin the process of defining the partner selection process with a set of design intents. These should include objectivity, criteria-based, strategically-driven, resource appropriate, multi-stepped and data-driven.

3 Develop and agree the selection process upfront, with particular focus on the criteria to be used at each of the gates, how many gates are needed, and how the gating criteria will be weighted.

4 At the first gate focus on the 12 key criteria and ensure that only information available from secondary data sources is needed.

5 At the final gate, include only two to four times as many companies as you will need in the ultimate collaboration. Add to the 12 key criteria the four additional measures of: similarity of values, common maturity, mutuality of benefit and style compatibility.

6 Only include on the short-list the actual preferred organization, or organizations if it is a multi-company collaboration.

7 Use the first phase of the collaboration establishment process described in Chapter 6 as the final go/no go decision for the collaboration to proceed.

CHAPTER 8

SHARED GOALS AND VALUES

A COMMON FRAMEWORK

Establishing common goals and values for a collaboration, draws upon the processes that many organizations employ to bring two firms together following a merger. Historic, embedded norms have to be replaced by a new set of operating parameters. Goals and values both exist to guide decision making within the collaboration entity. Goals provide direction and ambition, values provide the acceptable parameters within which these ambitions are achieved. It is important that goals and values, and also integrated planning and measurement (Chapters 9 and 10), all align with a common purpose. To make that happen, jointly agree a clear, consistent and linked framework.

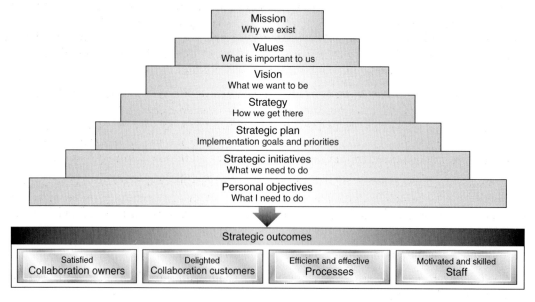

FIGURE 8.1: Strategic alignment framework

To build a common sense of purpose, agreement is required on a distinct mission (why the collaboration exists), a vision (what it is attempting to achieve) and the strategy, or more specifically, the strategic objectives or goals. The values also need to be agreed, but unlike the shared goals component, this is more about making values a reality in operation, rather than agreeing a set of statements on paper. We can begin by creating that common sense of purpose – how are a mission, vision and strategy devised for a collaboration?

SHARED GOALS

Some years before Armstrong took his first steps on the moon, NASA, the American Space Agency tasked with achieving this ambition, entertained a visit from J F Kennedy, the then president of the United States. While entering NASA's headquarters, J F Kennedy passed a cleaner who had come out to see the president on one of his walkabouts. The president asked the cleaner what it was that he did. Without thinking, the man replied 'My job is to help put a man on the moon'. A great example of vision deployed.

The converse was true of the British Prison Systems in the mid-1990s. Following a number of high profile worrying cases, the government ordered a review. A key conclusion from that study, the Learmont Report, stated the following,

> (Any organization which boasts one Statement of Purpose, one Vision, five Values, six Goals, seven Strategic Priorities and eight Key Performance Indicators without any clear correlation between them is producing a recipe for total confusion and exasperation.)

How is that sense of clarity achieved within a collaboration? The first step is to understand why the collaboration exists.

Why are we here? The mission

The mission of the collaboration describes its *raison d'être*, and it is critical to understand this if the scope of the collaboration is to remain focused. Collaborations will always have a higher level master – the organizations that decided to bring them into existence – and so they must operate within the boundaries given by their parent companies. If the collaboration which created the Eurofighter took an independent view of how to use its combined capability to further dominate the defence marketplace, it would undoubtedly be successful. However, it would also conflict with the mission for which it was created.

A helpful factor when considering the underlying reason for creation, is the statement of strategic need, and by direct result, the chosen collaboration model. If this is a proposition-based collaboration, the mission of the new entity must talk about new value propositions. That is, after all, why the collaboration was created. If instead it is a capability-based collaboration, the definition of that capability area must feature in its mission statement.

The mission does not need to dictate the collaboration's expected outcomes. That is a role retained for the vision. It does, however, need to set at the highest possible level, the statement of scope for the collaboration. Examples for each of the models of collaboration could be:

Supply chain collaboration

☐ To operate the lowest cost ambient supply chain within the North American market (food manufacturing).

☐ To deliver two-hour service provision for the European car aftermarket (automotive parts, MOT suppliers etc.).

Capability-based collaboration

☐ To be the leading player for digital technology solutions (electronics sector).

☐ To own the strongest brands in the telecommunications markets (telecommunications provider).

Proposition-based collaboration

☐ To bring innovation to clothes retailing (fashion house).

☐ To create the new generation of airline fleets (airplane manufacturing).

Competitive collaboration

☐ To dominate the high-end business banking sector (financial institution).

☐ To control internet access (ISP).

The mission provides a useful reminder to the collaboration's executive team of why they are there and what their legal remit is. It bounds the activities that they can perform. When a collaboration begins to operate outside of that arena, it can mean only one of three things:

1　The executive team have overstepped their remit, and need to be brought back into line.

2　The mission of the collaboration is wrong.

3　The reason for the collaboration's existence is no longer valid.

Refocusing the executives, or redefining the mission can remedy the first two of these problems. If the collaboration no longer fulfils its stated mission, a fundamental rethinking of the collaboration is needed. This could lead either to the dissolving of the collaboration, or to the evolving of the entity into a new form, for a new purpose.

Time-based aspiration – the vision

We know why we exist, but to what end? What is the collaboration attempting to achieve? The first rule of vision, and one that is absolutely pivotal for collaboration organizations, is that they are time-based. Collaborations are not necessarily created for all time. Most organizations do not set concrete strategic plans for their own organizations with a time horizon of greater than five years (high investment-based industries are a notable exception). Knowing what is needed and by when, brings the whole creation of the collaboration into focus. Take NASA, and our inspired cleaner. NASA's mission as an organization focuses on the exploration of space. That will stand for all time, or until the United States decides it does not require NASA. Back when J F Kennedy visited however, the vision of the organization was: 'To put a man on the moon by the end of the decade'. A clear end outcome (man on the moon), and a clear time frame by which to achieve it (the end of the 1960s).

For many organizations, a singular and clear focus is not always easy, although for a collaboration, clarity of vision is easier to achieve than in most cases. The founding parents have set up collaborations usually for a specific and defined purpose. If this is not the case, then perhaps they should not have been created. Although this model of outcome and time frame is not a strict rule for a collaboration vision, it is extremely helpful if this strategic tool is relevant to the collaboration, rather than an inspirational but non-specific statement, which vision can too often become.

Vision also benefits from qualification, using either a very important 'how' statement, or the qualification of boundaries. Almost two decades ago, Merck stated their vision: 'To establish Merck as the pre-eminent drug-maker worldwide in the 1980s' (National Defence University 'Strategic Vision' paper 1979). This provided time frame (by the end of 1989), geographical scope (global) and also outcome (pre-eminent). Perhaps outcome is the weakest element here, because pre-eminent could mean a great many things.

We can study each of the eight mission statements provided earlier, two for each model of collaboration. What appropriate vision statements could go hand in hand with these underlying reasons for existence?

Supply chain collaboration

☐ To achieve a cost of goods delivered below 7 per cent within three years (distribution costs as a percentage of sales).

☐ To meet our fulfilment standards on time, every time on the European continent by 2003.

Capability-based collaboration

☐ To achieve 25 per cent global market share of digital technology products by 2005.

☐ To be better known than Coca-Cola and McDonald's in North America by 2007.

Proposition-based collaboration

☐ To grow new range share to 30 per cent of overall revenue by 2006.

☐ To achieve over 40 per cent of new jumbo orders for delivery after 2010 for the world's top 30 airlines.

Competitive collaboration

☐ To be the chosen partner of six of the top 20 corporations, and to control 35 per cent of the total marketplace for business banking in the world's five major trading centres.

☐ To sign up one in two new internet customers from 2004.

What do all these proposed vision statements have in common? They are very specific, and in almost all cases, measurable. Many organizations do not take this approach to vision development, often because they feel that vision should be more 'aspirational' and less specific. However, if vision is to achieve its goal and provide precise, focused guidance to the collaboration organization, specific and measurable are powerful characteristics of the vision statement.

Take a mountain climber as an example. Climbing mountains is her mission (what she has chosen to do). Suppose that this climber has decided that her life-time dream is to climb Mount Everest. Her vision might be, for example, 'To reach the peak of Mount Everest before my 35th birthday'. Clearly defined, measurable, time-based. This does not mean that she cannot climb other mountains; it does mean that she knows exactly what drives her motivation and focus. When she has climbed Everest and achieved that vision, a new vision could be articulated. Perhaps to climb the peaks of the world's five highest mountains, or perhaps to climb Mount Everest in under four hours, or even to climb it unassisted (e.g. no oxygen). Today's vision does not in any way inhibit tomorrow's. And if this climber had a support team, they would be equally clear on what the goal was. Like the cleaner mopping the floor of NASA.

However, if our climber's vision statement had said 'To optimize recognized high altitude peak achievements through focused planning and execution', while this broadly says the same thing, it would not focus the mind nor the organization, on the fundamental dimension of success. Vision creates the clear framework to answer the question 'What are we here to achieve?', however, when that aspiration is translated to a specific set of shared goals, true clarity can be brought to the collaboration's role.

A common strategy – the goals

Vision identifies the star which we are travelling towards. The strategy is the map that tells us how to traverse the terrain between where we are and that visible, but distant, end point. At this level of goal congruence, we begin to understand how aligned the collaboration's founding organizations are.

There are many frameworks that can be used for this, and the balanced scorecard's approach, which considers financial, customer, internal process and innovation and learning is as useful a starting point as any. This four quadrant model is frequently adapted to be specifically relevant to the collaboration – a competitive collaboration may be more interested in market, than it is customer, a capability-based collaboration may wish to have a certain quadrant considering another focus, and so on.

The starting point for this strategy process is to build the statement of strategic need, within the context of the mission and vision. We are trying to take the strategic needs in each of the areas from the partner organizations, and agree a single statement that represents the needs of all firms in a particular area. For example, in a supply chain collaboration, one of the firms may be focused on delivering their products to the customer on time and at a low cost, while the other may be focused on using the collaboration to build a broad, scalable logistics network that allows them to take that infrastructure and sell it elsewhere. The goal statements for the collaboration need to explicitly meet these individual firms' strategic needs and to identify areas of conflict. Building an infrastructure demands investment and that will help to reduce unit cost and improve service performance for this collaboration. However, if one party has a use outside the collaboration for this improved capability via other third-party relationships, how does that work? There is a need to achieve goal congruence:

☐ Is it the goal of the collaboration to go and find other third parties to join the entity and share further cost efficiencies, or is it a secondary motive for one of the parties?

☐ Given the answer to this question, how should investment be shared, and what scope of the activities should be under the remit of the collaboration?

☐ What is the mission of the collaboration? To own an infrastructure or deliver product and service at low cost? Is this still correct, given a more granular discussion on this key point?

It is important in the development of goals, that an appropriate process is used to identify the implications of the strategic statement. This ensures that it is not an exercise in prose, but one of strategic clarity. Some simple tools can help to achieve this:

☐ **Goal alignment** – Simply ask all individuals in the group to rate, out of ten, whether the collaboration goal supports the statement of strategic need from each party.

☐ **Force field analysis** – For each statement, identify the list of drivers that will help that goal be achieved, and conversely the list of drivers that would oppose it being created. The drivers list can then be assessed to consider how likely they are to occur and the line of the force field can be drawn – either indicating success or failure.

☐ **Best hopes, worst fears** – For each statement, parties from each of the parent organizations identify their greatest hopes for what that goal statement could mean for their organization, and then their worst fears about how that statement could be 'abused' by other parties and result in a negative impact for their own organization. Sharing hopes and fears not only builds trust and openness, it feeds into the risk process and helps to ensure that well-intentioned goals do not drive inappropriate and unintended behaviours.

The vision, mission and strategy combine to give a sense of shared goals. We have clearly articulated where we are going and how we will get there. Nonetheless, that is only half of the process for laying the foundations of success. Can we work together? Do we have a set of shared values to work with?

SHARED VALUES

Firstly, what do we mean by values? Frequently when collaboration efforts go wrong, it is put down to 'a clash of values'. The French and English organizations that created the Eurotunnel struggled in their early days to be effective and blamed different values. When the might of Disney brought Florida-style entertainment to Paris, in the form of Euro Disney, to meet initially with failure, the reason was given that the trading values in France had not been fully understood by the Disney executives. What are these elusive values?

We can start with a definition. Values are the framework that enables managers and staff to make decisions aligned with the goals of the organization. These include both 'hard' and 'soft' decisions. The question of whether to invest in new warehouse facilities or the dilemma over how many days off, if any, to give a call centre operator whose mother has just died, can and should be guided by the values statement of the collaboration. Values are demonstrated through behaviour and decision making, not the ability to recant the ten chosen words that comprise the statement. How are values developed? Begin at the end and work back.

It is all about decisions

If collaboration has a delivery commitment of the same product to two customers but can only meet one order, which one does it service? If it has made the commitment to one customer, but another much larger and more strategic customer 'demands' a rush order, what one does it service? If the collaboration has committed to neither, but both put through an order, one being a long-standing customer and the other a 'spot' buyer, with the latter offering 20 per cent above normal list price, which one does it service? These questions can only be answered by knowing the values of the collaboration (i.e. what do we value?). Is customer loyalty more important than short-term profit? Is ethical trading seen as a better long-term value creation approach than short-term profit capture? Does partner commitment outweigh immediate returns? Rather than develop the values and then attempt to apply them, use these sort of questions to form the values – the process of doing so is as useful as the outcome it creates.

Use of scenarios

Begin by developing ten to 20 scenarios that reflect the sort of critical day-to-day dilemmas that the collaboration will face. This could include customer prioritization, staff management, investment decisions or planning assumptions. These scenarios need to cover:

☐ A business context.

☐ A specific business decision that is required.

☐ The constraints within which that decision needs to be made.

☐ The time frame within which the decision and associated action needs to be executed.

Teams, representing each of the collaboration partners, take a scenario, discuss as a group the way they would deal with it, and then each group shares their recommendations. Where common conclusions are reached, the underlying principles on which the decision was based can be captured. Where groups come to very different recommendations, debate why a different decision-making framework exists. What were the assumptions underpinning the conclusion? What priorities were placed on different decision-making criteria? Or to be more precise – what value statements were used to make that decision?

As each scenario is worked through, this list of values statements will develop. You will recognize that more and more decisions draw upon the same set of underlying assumptions. Where differences emerge, this tends to be for one of two reasons:

1   The inherent 'corporate style' is different.

2   There is no common understanding of the strategy.

The second one of these is easier to address. If, for example, two partners make a different decision about an investment option, that must be because a strategic goal is either not clear enough, or has been interpreted differently by each party. Rerunning the scenarios, this time with the set of strategic goals visible and each scenario linked back to the specific goal, can flush out where the wording of the goal needs to be refined. This may be because it is being interpreted differently, a goal is missing or there is no goal congruence and the goal alignment process in that particular area needs to be reworked. But what about corporate style? That is more challenging.

Corporate style

Culture is not a choice for an organization. A firm cannot decide to not have a culture. It exists regardless. The key question that organizations face is whether their cultures are created by design, or whether they form by default. For many, it is the latter. Sometimes the ethnic or national mix drives part of the culture; sometimes a very directive or inspirational chief executive or founder does; for some a hugely successful or highly traumatic corporate event (e.g. take-over, large-scale restructuring) achieves it. What is apparent is that it is not an exact science, and for those operating within a culture, many of its traits are invisible to them. For collaborations to work, while the values statement defines what is required in the new entity or across the partners, corporate style highlights the challenge to achieve that. Understanding this is the most important factor.

Corporate style can rarely be written down, and so it is a very perception-based area. Often two individuals will observe the exact same events, but describe the corporate style differently. The best way to tackle corporate style is to find ways to try and describe this perception.

A common and helpful model is the use of parallel descriptors. These could be animals, film stars, or just 'five adjectives'. Whichever model is used, the same six-step process is appropriate. Let us illustrate, using five adjectives:

1   Each collaboration partner says five adjectives that they feel best describe themselves.

2   Each partner then chooses five adjectives for each of the other partners.

3   Each partner then chooses five adjectives which describe how they think the other partners see them.

4   Each of these lists is shared with all parties. A set of underlying assumptions or perceptions is drawn up from the debate which follows the explanations of which words were chosen, why they were chosen, and how different the choice was for each organization.

5   Collectively, a list of potential pitfalls is developed, which flows from the discussion of differences. Specifically, how might the differences in corporate style show itself in actions and behaviours that could cause the collaboration to fail?

6   Finally, a new list is agreed upon that embodies the collective style that the collaboration should demonstrate, and the transition path for each partner is identified.

Whether animals, cars, personalities, cartoons or words are used, the process is powerful and puts the perception clearly on the table. This makes the process of debate around style an acceptable agenda item on an ongoing basis.

Embedding values

The processes of scenario-based values development and parallel descriptors both begin to make values a way of working and not just a theoretical exercise. However, embedding that model of operation is an ongoing process. There are a number of tools to help achieve this, but the three most useful ones include: creating legends, role-based guiding principles and values champions.

Creating legends – Folklore is a powerful base for building values. Organizational legends. These are created through some form of discontinuity, and normally involve an over-response to a specific event that demonstrated a particular value in an extreme way. That response may be at an individual level: a middle manager who is suddenly catapulted onto the board, or conversely an existing executive who is fired and walked off the premises for a clear breach of values. It may be at a team level, for instance, a team off-site visit to Bermuda is given for outstanding performance, or a substantive cash payment. Or it could even be in the marketplace: trading has ceased with a major customer because they constrain the organization from trading in line with its values. The only common characteristic is that the reaction is extreme; such that the most powerful communication mechanism in the organization – the grapevine – is in overdrive.

Role-based guiding principles – At a more practical level, values statements can be too high level to actually guide daily choices, particularly further down the business. Role-based guiding principles can overcome this. The guiding principles can either be a separate document, or a section heading within the job description template. Either way, it contains for each of the major roles some example descriptors of how each of the values could be exhibited within that role. For example, a collaboration value of 'Being commercially focused in everything that we do', could be translated to a purchase ledger clerk through actions such as: identifying suppliers who have trading terms more generous than the company standard and changing them; or proactively asking suppliers paid through traditional methods to move to electronic transfer. A corporate desire made practical, specific and applicable to even the simplest of roles. If the focus of role-based values can be brought into the induction process, then a foundation for their effective implementation can be created.

Values champions – Who owns the values? Strategic goals often have executives' names cleared marked against them. However, who worries about the fact that the stated value of customer focus is achieved? Too often, nobody. This demonstrates the value of creating values champions. Individuals are explicitly tasked to ensure values goals come off paper and become part of the fabric of how the collaboration operates. Values champions have the same challenge to be effective as the process owner model – they have been given accountability and authority, in a particular area, to direct, reward and discipline staff who do not work for them directly. Values champions is a non-hierarchical concept – if the chief executive is a culprit, the same process has to be applied – even if he or she is your boss. The concept of values champions is not without its challenges. However, in the same way that many organizations have made process owners work, with clear ground rules and the collective agreement of the collaboration board, someone who worries about values becoming an operational reality across the collaboration workforce, can be a powerful ally.

SUMMARY

1 Creating a common sense of purpose for the collaboration requires a single, integrated framework covering mission, vision, strategy and values. This framework can then guide the integrated planning and measurement model.

2 Mission defines the *raison d'être* of the collaboration, and is a useful tool to control its scope.

3 Vision outlines the effective outcome of the collaboration, and is most useful if it is time-based, outcome-driven and qualifies the outcome in terms of geography, customer group or market. It should be easier for a collaboration to identify a clear vision than for its parent organizations as it has been set up for a defined purpose.

4 Goals, or strategic objectives, are the most useful level at which to ensure congruence across the partners. They will often use a balanced scorecard framework comprising of financial, customer, internal process and innovation and learning quadrants. However, any other appropriate grouping of goals is equally helpful.

5 Values statements are best developed by taking real-life scenarios and using them to identify and debate differences of view about what decisions should be made to resolve those scenarios.

6 The use of parallel descriptors, such as adjectives, animals, personalities or cartoons is a useful way to understand relative perceptions about the corporate styles of the organizations participating in the collaboration.

7 Ensuring that values become embedded within the collaboration is challenging, but can be helped by appointing values champions, creating role-based guiding principles and by creating 'legends'.

8 The overall test of success for both goals and values is that they are pragmatic and specific, not conceptual or generic.

CHAPTER 9

INTEGRATED PLANNING

MAKING IT MEASURABLE

What will make the aspiration of the collaboration an operational reality? We know the mission, vision, strategy and values – we know all of the *whats*, but what about the *how*? How do we translate collaboration goals into a mechanism that can deliver the expected returns to the parent organizations? Making the strategy measurable is the critical first step. The role of measurement is best described by two well-known adages:

- [ ] What you measure is what you get.

- [ ] If you can measure it, you can manage it.

We finished our exercise on shared goals and values with a set of strategic objectives that define the aspiration of the collaboration, have as their over-arching statement the vision, and which underpin and support the mission. Now we have to take these to the next level of definition – a performance measurement. But how?

Do Wells

Leaping directly from an objective statement to a measurement can lead to a number of problems, the most common of which is individuals following a different thought process and set of assumptions. Enter the concept of 'Do Wells'. Do Wells provide a transparent mechanism by which the move from objective to measurable target can be achieved. Consider the example of a collaboration that exists to build the network infrastructure for a national utility. The objective statement could say something like: 'To build the agreed infrastructure by achieving new levels of capital efficiency'. What does that actually mean? The best way to answer that is to ask: 'What do we have to Do Well if we are going to achieve that stated objective?' The Do Wells for this objective are likely to include:

- [ ] Be realistic in our planning approach and time-scales.

- [ ] Complete all work on time.

☐ Have workforce flexibility.

☐ Be excellent at project management.

☐ Utilize effective capital planning tools.

☐ Ensure stock forecasting is accurate.

☐ Align design standards across projects.

☐ Effectively manage contract labour.

☐ Purchase raw materials at competitive unit costs.

☐ Ensure on time availability of all network parts.

☐ Be able to clearly benchmark historic capital efficiency performance.

☐ Have a competitive pay structure for all resources building the network.

☐ Build good relationships with the planning authorities.

☐ Engage local public concern groups.

The Do Wells provide the structure to ensure a common understanding of the stated business objective. They are also the 'audit trail' to help explain to others why particular measurements have been chosen to articulate a certain business goal. Once we know the Do Wells, we must translate them into performance measures.

There are a number of characteristics that define good measures, and in particular there are three that can provide a framework. These are balancing lead and lag, ensuring controllability and considering behaviours.

Balancing lead and lag – Lag indicators tell us, after the event, whether we achieved a goal or not. These tend to be most closely linked to the goal statement itself. For the example of the national utility collaboration building the infrastructure, the most appropriate lag indicator for capital efficiency will be a capital efficiency index. In other words, if 100 is the baseline cost, against which we previously built capital projects, can we build this new network for less than 100? We may, for example, set a target of 85. If the infrastructure is a homogeneous network, then the measure may be cost per kilometre or cost per unit of output. This will tell us whether we have achieved that objective statement or not, but it does little to warn us in advance if we are likely to achieve it. Lag measures are the equivalent of spilt milk and crying. Necessary to understand achievement; but they can be futile to drive actions. Hence the critical importance of lead indicators and the role of Do Wells.

What can we measure to let us know if the capital efficiency measure is going to come in on target or not? These are lead indicators. Monitoring the cost of raw material when it is bought is probably helpful, particularly if this is a major percentage of the capital cost. If this month's procurement is higher than planned, when we capitalize a project on its completion six months down the line, it is likely it will have a poor efficiency level. Similarly for resources. If we use contract labour at a higher cost than imagined, it will show further down the line as higher capital cost. Getting planning permission on time will impact the roll-out schedule, and with it costs. This might be a very useful lead indicator that can give early warning about an eventual overrun to the network build. More importantly, with that level of visibility, management action can be taken to ensure that resolution before it impacts on the final, lag, indicator.

Ensuring controllability – Measurements are a good tool to focus accountability. Functions, teams or individuals need to own measures. Sometimes, high-level lag indicators may belong collectively to the collaboration board, for instance, market share for a proposition-based collaboration or delivered unit cost for a supply chain collaboration. It is a priority, regardless of where the particular measure sits, that the individual or group with accountability for that target, controls enough of the delivery levers to take on its ownership. Two things will happen if this rule is not applied:

1 Insufficient management action can be taken if the measure begins to be missed.

2 Team or individual motivation dips when they are perceived to be non-performing and yet have no ability to remedy the issue.

Returning again to our capital efficiency metric, if the collaboration building the network sources the raw materials from one of the partner companies at predetermined prices, and raw materials comprise 80 per cent of the capital cost, this measurement will prove unhelpful to the collaboration. It cannot change the raw material costs, the other cost elements are insignificant, and therefore it is inappropriate to apply this measure. On time roll-out may be appropriate. Non-material capital efficiency may be appropriate. Raw material utilization (i.e. low levels of write-offs or scrap) may be appropriate. However, capital efficiency is too high level and out of the control of the collaboration to be useful.

The decision on controllability needs to be based on some core assumptions. In most areas of business, collaboration or otherwise, there will be some elements outside the control of the individual or group managing the measurement. The weather may have a significant impact on the collaboration's ability to meet its dates. However, this is uncontrollable to all parties. The simple test of influence is the percentage of controllable drivers that the collaboration can impact.

Considering behaviours – Customer loyalty is a common objective, particularly for supply chain collaborations from a service perspective and for proposition-based collaborations from a differentiation perspective. How do we measure loyalty? Order frequency and customer churn are commonplace indicators. However, these are lag, so what might be lead? Most organizations accept the relationship between customer satisfaction and customer loyalty, and a good test for dissatisfaction is customer complaints, which could be a useful lead indicator. Or is it?

Whether complaints are a good indicator or not depends on what behaviours they drive. Remember – what you measure is what you get. What management actions can be taken to reduce the number of complaints? One is clearly to reduce the causes for complaints, such as late deliveries, defects or poor service, but there are other actions that can be taken. Complaints tend to come into the collaboration at all levels and types. Recording them on the complaints system carries with it a measure of interpretation. An equally likely behaviour that results from measuring complaints could be that the number of complaints falls, due to lower reporting, rather than to an underlying improvement.

A test of a good measure is that it will drive the right behaviours. In this situation, two paths forward could be followed:

1 Change the measure to something that is more independent. For example, a third-party conducted rolling customer satisfaction survey.

2   Consider the consequences that should go with the measure to ensure that behaviours are correct. We might decide that more complaints is positive, and that the additional measure to monitor is the speed with which they are resolved and the customer's satisfaction with the given solution.

DEFINING DEPLOYMENT LEVERS

Through the use of measures, strategic statements are transformed into precise and specific targets that define success for the collaboration. We have to make sure that we can achieve those targets, which require a plan that uses all of the necessary levers at our disposal. These levers are the resources of the collaboration processes, technology, people and capability, structure and governance, management and reporting, and relationships.

Deployment of the objectives and measures needs to ascertain two things:

1   Which of these levers needs to be used to achieve the stated goals?

2   What degree of change is needed to that lever if the collaboration goals are to be met?

This deployment can be conducted using a simple matrix.

Processes

Processes describe the work architecture or in simpler terms, the full list of tasks and activities conducted by the organization. In supply chain collaborations, processes are the most critical deployment lever, but they will have an important role to play in all models of collaboration. The role of process to enable strategy typically focuses on, firstly, the capacity (volume) and capability (service/quality) of any process managed by the collaboration and, secondly, the process interfaces. Each process will clearly identify the inputs and outputs, and how those key elements need to be managed. For collaborations, such as competitive or proposition-based, the focus on process interfaces is key. The entity of the collaboration conducts very few tasks itself, and therefore a priority is to ensure that the inputs it receives from either partner organizations or other third parties will deliver the marketplace promise of the collaboration.

Technology

Chapters 2–5 discussed the role of technology in each of the different forms of collaboration model. This may vary from full Enterprise Resource Planning (ERP) and value chain collaboration tools, to simple sharing of common reporting. To understand how technology will support the strategy, it is important to see how it underpins and supports the processes the collaboration will use, and how the technology touch points at the interface of the collaboration and other parties are managed in a similar way to the process inputs and outputs. For technology, these inputs and outputs are most likely to focus on data and information, rather than process components.

People and capability

Strategic goals need resources to deliver them. How many and at what skill level? The deployment of strategic goals can guide this. It can also clarify exactly what each of the partners puts into the collaboration, and what delivery mechanisms are managed from within the collaboration entity or supplied to it from parent organizations. Collaboration endeavours frequently exhibit the same test of commitment that internal change programs do. Those

STRATEGIC OBJECTIVE ⟋ IMPLEMENTATION LEVERS	OBJECTIVE 1	OBJECTIVE 2	OBJECTIVE 3	OBJECTIVE 4	OBJECTIVE 5	OBJECTIVE 6	OBJECTIVE 7	OBJECTIVE 8
PROCESS								
TECHNOLOGY								
PEOPLE AND CAPABILITY								
STRUCTURE AND GOVERNANCE								
MANAGEMENT AND REPORTS								
RELATIONSHIPS								

TABLE 9.1: Deployment matrix example

leading either effort will demand that the organization's 'best people' are needed to make the concept work – for some this request is met in full, for others a collection of individuals who are unassigned, 'between roles' or 'taking a sideways move for development reasons' are provided. This is a pitfall to beware of.

Structure and governance

Usually, in the collaboration establishment process, the first level of governance has been defined by this point. Measures, or more specifically, the accountability for them, are a helpful mechanism to test the governance's appropriateness and to finish the lower level structures. If there is an underlying assumption that each strategic objective and supporting measure need to be owned by somebody, the ability to assign them into the proposed governance model is a good test of its logic. This also helps to confirm that the governance groups, such as the collaboration board and other lower level structures, know what they are there to manage and monitor.

Management and reporting

Management control is a critical, but often forgotten, resource of a collaboration, or any other organization for that matter. Ensuring that the people, technology and processes are in place to achieve a strategic goal answers any resource question, but is this enough to ensure success? Do those have the right incentives? Is there competent management supervision? Do team leaders have the operational reporting they need to know that their part of the collaboration is on track? These are important questions to ask to ensure that the glue holding the resource elements of the collaboration is in place.

Relationships

Almost all collaborations have some form of symbiotic relationship with the organizations that created them. In the case of most types of supply chain or capability-based collaborations, this relationship is constant at an operational and day-to-day level. For others, the touch points are more strategic and decision-based, but as a result even more critical if they are to succeed. The collaboration executives need to ensure that these relationships are seen as both a resource and as a critical interface to be expertly managed. There is a 'hard' element to this in the form of the legal contracts, risk and reward models and so on, but also a 'soft' element, such as drawing on expertise, tools, *ad hoc* resources and market intelligence. When collaborations are formed, the relationship is often very one way – the 'parent' firms send instructions down. As the collaboration entity takes on a life of its own, this must become a two-way process, which the collaboration uses to ensure that its mission and vision can be achieved.

LEFT TO RIGHT INTEGRATED PLANNING

We clearly understand our goals and measures. We have identified all of the elements of our resources that are needed to deliver those targets and now we just need to do the plan – the integrated plan. Chapter 6 discussed the fundamental difference between addressing known problems (continuous improvement) and unconstrained opportunities (step changes). Ensuring that both elements get full attention and are initially addressed independently in the planning process is important. The role of the measures and the targets attached to them, provide overall guidance in terms of how much of the prize can be delivered by improving what we can already see, compared to how much radical thinking is needed.

The priority is to make sure that the whole plan links together. This can be challenging. Typically the known opportunities tend to be quite bounded, based on known information and carry with them a high probability of being achieved. The step-change ideas typically carry more risk, are based on assumption more than fact, and are likely to have a more variable level of success. Yet there must only be one plan.

Here again, the deployment levers can provide a helpful framework to provide this single picture. If the deployment levers are the resources that can be utilized to achieve the goals, aligning the plan under those headings makes sense. In many ways, the integrated plan activities become the flip side of the coin to the measures deployment matrix that started the process. This is where we return to measures.

All of the measurements we have used so far have focused on ensuring that we know whether we have achieved or will achieve the collaboration's strategic aims. The planning process has provided the list of actions collectively deemed necessary to make the goals a reality. Monitoring the achievement of that plan is perhaps the best lead indicator of all. The plan's underlying assumption is that if all its actions are completed on time, all of the strategic goals will be met. Therefore, if we were 100 per cent confident in that assumption, we would not need to monitor output or strategic measures at all. We could simply measure the activities to check they have happened, and live in the comfort that by default our outcome aims had been met.

In reality of course, planning assumptions never carry this level of confidence, particularly where step-change actions have been developed. The very process of reviewing the relationship between planned activities, their assumed impact on the outcome measures, and the actual impact is a critical learning process, and one that we will cover in more detail in Chapter 10.

There is one final step to complete this plan, which also informs the targets on the outcome measures. Time. Our planning process may have delivered a list of initiatives or activities that are necessary to achieve the collaboration's strategic goals, but we cannot do them all at once. Some actions may rely on others to happen first, before they can occur. Others may need to be conducted together. A few may be absolute precursors, without which the collaboration itself cannot get off the ground. Therefore, prioritizing the potential actions is extremely important.

OPPORTUNITY PRIORITIZATION

For an integrated plan to be useful, the activities need to be grouped into logical chunks of work that can be evaluated. A task list of 1000 activities is not helpful. A set of 20–30 key implementation 'mini-projects' or opportunities, is the basis for a robust, easy to understand and manageable plan – one around which prioritization can happen, and linkages can be identified.

Before prioritizing this list, an initial evaluation needs to assess if any of the opportunities are 'must dos', either because they are required for basic legal operation or they are precursors to anything else happening. Contracts, governance, health and safety, employment conditions and facilities will often fall into this category. That prioritization is easy – they must all be done first! After that, two rules guide the prioritization process:

1 **The 'bang for your buck' rule** – Or to be precise, do things that have the best balance of cost/time to accomplish and to impact on strategic goals.

2 **The mobilization rule** – Consider the timing on the plan. Deliverables that are visible, demonstrate progress, and will build confidence both within the collaboration and across the parent organizations should be time-phased appropriately.

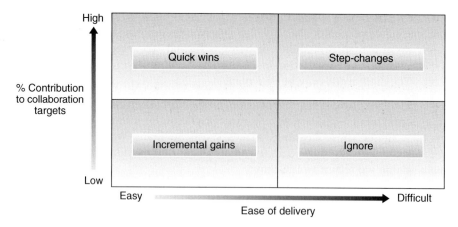

FIGURE 9.1: Collaboration prioritization matrix

Once the prioritization matrix has provided the direction, a time-based integrated plan for the collaboration can be constructed, and with it the phasing of the targets against the strategic measures. As critical projects deliver, the subsequent improvement in the performance against strategic measures should be seen.

SUMMARY

1 The starting point for an integrated plan is to translate the strategic goals into a set of performance measures which quantify their achievement.

2 The step from objective to measure is best achieved by identifying what the collaboration must Do Well if the objective is to be attained – this then defines the measures.

3 Each objective should have both lag indicators which confirm whether the goal was met, and lead indicators, which provide warning that the output goal could be missed.

4 The strategic measures need to be assigned to teams or individuals in such a manner that assignees have control over the majority of the drivers that enable achievement.

5 Measures need to be chosen based on the behaviours they are likely to drive, and a consequences process established which further reinforces these desired behaviours.

6 The strategic measures form the basis for deployment into the key planning levers of process, technology, people and capability, structure and governance, management and reporting and relationships.

7 The integrated plan combines both known opportunities (continuous improvement) with unconstrained opportunities (step change). Clear actions are identified to achieve the collaboration targets.

8 Activities identified by this planning exercise should be grouped into a set of identifiable opportunities, which can then be prioritized based on ease of delivery and contribution to the strategic goals.

9 The output is a single plan which brings together:

☐ Incremental and step-change opportunities.

☐ Linkages and dependencies between the opportunities.

☐ A time-phasing, which achieves targets early and delivers visible quick wins.

☐ Opportunity delivery with the timing of target setting, against the strategic measures.

CHAPTER 10

MEASUREMENT AND PERFORMANCE MANAGEMENT

THE MEASUREMENT MODEL

What is the measurement model? It is a single, interlinked set of performance measures that reach up into the vision and down into the lowest level of operational performance indicators. It covers all areas of activity for the collaboration and builds root cause into its design. Putting in place a measurement model follows a simple five-step process:

1 Confirm the strategic measures.

2 Conduct key driver analysis.

3 Complete lower level measure deployment.

4 Conduct a 'bottom up' process and plan check.

5 Build the data dictionary.

Level 1 Confirm the strategic measures

We should already have defined our strategic measures. To ensure that they are ready and appropriate to provide the framework on which to build the measurement model, there are some simple tests that can be applied. Assuming all of the tests are passed, we are in a position to proceed and build the model. If any tests are not passed, the activities need to be undertaken to proceed with building the model. The key questions that require a positive response are:

☐ Do all strategic objectives have measures that define them?

☐ Do all strategic objectives have both lead and lag measures that define them?

☐ Do the strategic objectives cover all elements of the collaboration's scope?

☐ Do the strategic objectives cover the spectrum of performance areas (e.g. use the balanced scorecard quadrants as a test for this)?

☐ Is there a clear definition (formula) for each of the performance measures?

☐ Has it been agreed who is accountable for each of these higher level measures, and therefore who will own its deployment in the measurement model?

☐ Has the set of strategic measures been approved by the collaboration board?

Once this set of measures is clearly understood, agreed and allocated we can begin to build the model from beneath them.

Level 2 Conduct key driver analysis

Measures are used in two ways to create the model:

1 Through organizational decomposition.

2 Through root cause, or key driver analysis.

Let us consider organizational decomposition – it is simplest to achieve and will comprise only a small percentage of the strategic measures. Suppose that one of the top level measures for the collaboration talks about the motivation and morale of the staff that are seconded into the collaboration. We may have decided that a simple way of measuring morale from a lag point of view is staff attrition rate. We will therefore need to track this as a whole for the collaboration. If, however, the staff working in the collaboration work within one of four departments, we may wish to channel that measure into each of these four areas. By doing this, if the attrition target for the collaboration is missed, we can immediately drill down and see whether this is a problem across the board, or specifically in one or two departmental areas.

Organizationally deployed measures are useful to identify where an issue sits within the collaboration structure, and this is particularly helpful for large collaborations, such as whole entity models, but it has not yet told us why the problem exists. Hence the need and major focus on root cause based deployment. To achieve this, we use key driver analysis.

For example, a top level objective for a supply chain collaboration may be to have the lowest stock levels in the sector, and the measure may be stock days (i.e. the number of days of sales that current stock levels provide). What we need to answer is 'What drives stock levels?' Typically, the key drivers would include:

☐ Accuracy of the sales forecast.

☐ Accuracy of the Materials Resource Planning (MRP) or planning tool (manual or automated) that converts the sales forecast into stock component requirements.

☐ Service level standard (fulfilment rate and delivery time-scale) committed to customers.

☐ Defect rate (stock reject rate).

☐ On time delivery rate from suppliers.

☐ Average lead time from suppliers.

☐ On time ordering to suppliers.

☐ Levels of obsolescence or write-offs.

☐ Stock count accuracy.

☐ Level of 'pipeline stock' (sitting on logistics vehicles, local stockholding units or channels).

This list of key drivers applies the principles of brainstorming, in the sense that we are trying to recognize all possible root causes. Once that list has been completed, the pareto approach (the principle that 80 per cent of anything can be dealt with in 20 per cent of the time) needs to be taken to decide what will go into the measurement model. Evidently, each top level measure cannot have 20–30 measures sitting beneath it, and for most performance measures three to four main root cause reasons will explain the performance gap in 80 per cent of situations. Therefore, a percentage needs to be assigned to each of the items on the list to identify our hypothesized view about the likelihood of that particular driver being the reason for a performance gap to occur, with the list totalling 100 per cent.

For each of these key drivers, we now need to find a performance measure that defines its success. Given that these are not the strategic measures, but are by definition lead indicators of strategic measures, we only need to identify one measure of that key driver. For most, it will be extremely easy to understand what that measure should be because key driver statements tend to imply a performance measure in their wording.

Although this deployment through key drivers to Level 2 measures will be carried out by the owners of the Level 1 measures, it is important that a check is carried out across all of the Level 2 measures. This will often highlight that there may be the same Level 2 measures, which explain or support multiple Level 1 measures. This is an entirely acceptable outcome. All that needs to happen at this point is that they are identified and when the data dictionary is produced at the final step of the model build, we will not create multiple definitions of the same measure. Check at this point if any two groups deploying measures have formed the same key driver, yet chosen slightly different measures to monitor it. If so, consensus should be gained on the correct, single measure. Again, this supports the principle of the same measures, delivered in a common manner and using the same formula.

Level 3 Complete lower level measure deployment

Before continuing, it is useful to assign the Level 2 measures. This keeps alignment between the measures model and organization structure, and also recognizes how much further deployment is needed. If by Level 2, measures have already been set that the front-line staff will be monitoring, there may be no need to go any further. If conversely, there are still several organization levels to go, then deployment may be a substantive exercise.

By conducting an organization check at this point, the issue of control is put squarely on the table. If we have developed measures and it is hard to find roles to own them, provided that the key driver analysis is correct, it highlights that there may be a problem with the organizational structure. If that structure does not allow for individuals to feel ownership of the stated strategic goals of the collaboration, what is the structure trying to achieve?

Continued lower level deployment again follows the two elements of root cause (key driver analysis) and organizational deployment. When fully complete, it should be clear what each individual, team and department within the collaboration should be focused on achieving, and they should understand what contribution is expected of them.

Level 4 Conduct a 'bottom up' process and plan check

We have focused so far on a top-down approach. This is essential because of the strategic focus of all collaborations, and the need to ensure that scope is tightly managed towards the mission of the entity. However, there are two other areas that need to be tested at this point:

1   Have some basic operational measures, needed to run some of the processes within the collaboration, been missed?

2   Does the integrated plan provide actions for all areas where improvement is needed?

A purchase ledger manager will want to monitor efficiency (invoices processed per person per day), speed (on time payment record, red letters) and quality (number of correct journal entries) to effectively run his or her team. This is regardless of the strategic agenda and irrelevant to the mission and vision of the collaboration. It is just what you need to do to run a good purchase ledger department.

Frequently, functions such as these, which can be described as 'strategically independent', do not sit within the boundaries of a collaboration, apart from in a whole entity model. If it is not the purchase ledger, areas such as sales, marketing and operations all have performance measures that are merely about running the day-to-day activities in an efficient and error-free manner. What do we do with these? We could choose to not measure them, or to create a separate measurement system for the more ordinary, operational performance standards. Clearly, both of these options are wrong. All measures, even operational ones, should support a strategic objective. If there is a stated goal around cost optimization, or cost efficiency, our purchase ledger manager's measures of invoices per person per day sits in that area. However, this is the point where a 'bottom up' check across all the supervisory and middle management level is helpful to ensure that there is a single measurement system for the collaboration, not multiple ones. Therefore, everything that defines success for the collaboration, at whatever level, is held in a single repository of performance reporting.

The second check we can do relates back to the integrated plan. Greater detail in terms of performance measures can provide greater focus on the necessary activities to ensure they are achieved. The integrated plan focused on the strategic performance measures. This is appropriate and allows initiatives to be developed that can be prioritized and interfaced in a sensible way. It is now helpful to take the lower level of granularity, probably the Level 2 measures, and apply a cross-check to the integrated plan. Is there anything in the measurement model that does not have an initiative to ensure it is achieved? Sometimes, when we look at the root causes issues, rather than the strategic outcome, it identifies gaps in the plan that can now be filled.

Level 5 Build the data dictionary

The focus here is on the lowest common denominator: the data item. The entire measurement model needs to be translated into a single document, which defines each set of data within the model and where that data will be sourced from. Is it legacy systems sitting somewhere in one of the parent organizations? Is it transaction systems the collaboration will operate? Is it third-party data sources? Is it a manual input? While we design the measurement model from the top and work down, we build it from the bottom and aggregate up.

In many cases, the measures themselves are not actually raw data items, but the outcome of two or more base data items, manipulated through a formula or algorithm to provide something useful for the collaboration managers. However, to build the measures, we must know the data. The cross-check across measures is important here. It is not uncommon for one piece of base data to feed 20 or 30 specific measures as seen by the collaboration. These may be the same measure but at different levels of the organization, or simply feeding into different formula. A good example is number of staff. There may be a range of measures that use this as a denominator to a productivity or cost measure – revenue/full time equivalent (FTE), average salary cost/FTE, staff leaving/total FTE are three simple examples.

The one priority to develop the data dictionary is rigour. Precisely how do we define that item of data? Specifically which system will it come from, and what is that item of data called within that system? Where can it be found, and who is accountable for managing the quality of that underlying data item?

Once the data dictionary is built and agreed by the board, four things are known, which comprise the foundation for building the technology system to deliver the data:

1   What items of data are needed and where to source them.

2   How the data feeds into each of the measures.

3   How the measures relate to one another through a hierarchical pyramid.

4   Who needs to see which of the measures on a routine basis.

GUIDING PRINCIPLES

Collaborations struggle with a whole range of integration issues. This can result in an alignment of operations, behaviours and decision making back towards the parent organizations, and away from making the new entity a success. Corporate values, different pay policies and alternative approaches to key business processes help to cause division, not commonality. The measurement model is critical because it is the very foundation on which a new, common culture and operational practice is based. It also takes emotion out of performance, by putting lucid facts on the table.

Another reason why the measurement model must be a precursor to the collaboration beginning its operation is strategic focus. Most organizations spend their time battling with the legacy of history. Working practices, human resource policies and procedures, management styles and local variation all evolve over decades and bring with them cultures and values that are not those desired for the new world. For a collaboration, none of these issues need exist. It is a new entity, where all elements of its operation can be purposefully designed. In addition, the collaboration exists for a focused and specific purpose – almost like a project. The mission and vision provide the over-arching statements for scope and rationale, and the measurement model ensures that every individual working within the collaboration understands this level of strategic focus and that the agreed resources under the control of the collaborative venture are marshalled in the same direction.

Constructing this measurement model can be assisted by bearing in mind eight guiding principles that govern its role and application:

1   Define the performance measures by using the strategic objectives developed as part of the transformation design and planning phase of collaboration establishment.

2 All other measures used within the collaboration must be aligned and directly support this set of top level measures. If they do not, either they will drive focus away from the strategic intent of the collaboration, or the initial set of strategic measures is incomplete.

3 Build a new measurement system for the collaboration. While in almost every other area the collaboration will 'steal' tools, approaches and even infrastructure from its parent companies, the measures model is the one thing that should be uniquely designed for the sole purpose of the collaboration.

4 Clearly link the organization structure of the collaboration to the agreed measures, so that it is clear who monitors which group of measures. Where appropriate combine these into role or governance group-based reports. It is paramount to ensure that all the individuals, particularly where they come from different parent organizations, who conduct the same role, get the same sets of information.

5 Define and agree a single data source for each measure. Frequently the same area of reporting is fed by different data sources, often sourced from the different collaboration partners' organizations. It is key that everyone in the collaboration views the same set of performance information using the same sets of data, thus the performance conversation can be about improvement, not challenging data quality.

6 Apply modern reporting technology. Since the 1990s, the improvements in database and data warehouse technology have been vast. In parallel, the costs for such systems have fallen dramatically. If there is one place where investment is necessary for the collaboration, it is in underpinning database support.

7 Create a separate team that focuses on the process of managing the measures model and the provision of reporting. This is not a finance function task, although ultimately the team may reside in finance. It is about integrated measurement and reporting across the whole collaboration, and it needs a performance management team (or individual) to ensure the process achieves its goal.

8 Make sure the measures model is designed around root causes evaluation. Repeatedly, when performance falls below expected targets, it triggers an investigation into why. If the measures model is designed effectively, the root causes component is already built into the model, allowing immediate identification and resolution of poor performance.

TECHNOLOGY OPTIONS

All there is to do now is build it. Simple. In one way yes, but the challenge is the choice. An effective measurement model can be delivered via technology costing a hundred thousand dollars or one costing several million. So how do we choose? What is the difference between such a broad range of prices? Is the more expensive solution better? Considering five design principles of the measurement system can help to provide clarity.

Delivery interface

How does the collaboration wish to receive this measurement information? Few organizations operate through weekly or monthly paper reports and it is unlikely that any collaboration would choose to do this. Is it through the collaboration intranet the information will be observed, or by accessing the reporting system, or simply by navigating back into transactional systems? How important is the user interface? Does the presentation layer need to be highly intuitive and visually appealing, or is accuracy of data all that matters?

Time criticality

How important is real-time data? Given that whatever reporting tool is chosen, data will almost inevitably be sucked from legacy systems of some description, the difference between an overnight one-way batch interface, versus a real-time two-way interface is significant. The only way to address this issue in an informed way, is to understand the cost equation. Evidently, real time is favourable to delayed, but how critical is that issue? Would business decisions be made differently if the information is 12 hours old? Often that question cannot be answered at a macro-level. For items such as product availability, real time may be a commercial necessity. For others, such as productivity numbers or customer satisfaction, daily is more than adequate.

User manipulation

What do users want to see? Predefined measures, or the data that comprises it to further investigate trends, correlations and root cause items? With the evolution of data warehousing and the intuitive nature of its use, the power of information is placed increasingly into the hands of managers. Frequently, what is wanted is a set of standard reports that each manager can access in an automated way, and 'data cubes' which contain the key performance data for their area of the collaboration, which can be investigated further.

Data ownership

This area will have the greatest impact on the server infrastructure needed to support the measurement model. Does the collaboration wish to store all of the underlying data within its measurement system? Sometimes the legal basis of the collaboration dictates, at least in part, the answer to this question. Accessing data from parent organizations may not be an acceptable structure. Also, going forward, will the collaboration create and store all of its own data, or is it still 'piggybacking' transactional systems from other parties?

Staff access

Who can see what? The measurement model is built around upward and downward cascade. It is the most critical design principle of the whole creation. Executives can drill down where performance targets are missed and identify root cause, supervisors can aggregate up and see how their part of the operation supports the overall strategic goals. However, is that needed? Or indeed, is that allowed? Are there elements of the model where the performance information is sensitive? Should access be limited to certain parts of it? Are there strategic measures that only the collaboration board are allowed to see? Is there a philosophy that considers open access to all elements distracting?

By answering these questions on user delivery interface, time criticality, user manipulation, data ownership and staff access, the specification of the system can be defined. An increasingly common technology for collaborative endeavours is, however, the user of Portal technology. Able to access legacy systems, spreadsheets, manual input and also the core data repository, Portal technology is a presentation layer that provides high user interactivity and accessibility, without trying to overcome all of the challenges of interfaces, data migration and the like. And it can be applied quickly – often a critical imperative for a collaboration. When the Portal is in place, the data provision that happens beneath it can move into a single, common data repository, making the delivery more robust and future proof. This is all invisible to the user community, who receive a completely common and integrated measurement tool from day one of the collaboration's operation.

PERFORMANCE MANAGEMENT

Measurement is fine. However, it is how those measures are used to close performance gaps and drive improvement that matters. This is where the Plan-Do-Review cycle becomes the cornerstone of collaboration operations. Uncomplicated in design, but demanding absolute rigour and discipline in operation, Plan-Do-Review is the management model.

Plan

Why do we need to plan?

☐ Proactive work is between five and ten times cheaper than reactive work.

☐ To minimize the conflict between activities.

☐ To make the most of potential synergies between activities.

☐ To reduce delays and reactive activity.

☐ To increase productivity (i.e. achieve more with the same resources).

☐ To ensure resources are available.

Key inputs to the 'plan' element of the cycle:

☐ Budgets.

☐ Objectives, targets and key performance indicators (KPI).

☐ Schedules of activities, tasks or jobs.

Do

Do represents the operations of the business:

☐ Procedures, policies, work instructions.

☐ Work and business processes.

☐ Consumes resources – people, cash, tools, raw materials.

☐ Often controlled and managed with tools such as the ISO 9000:2000 quality management standard.

Key inputs to the 'do' element of the cycle:

☐ Detailed/low level plans.

☐ Priorities deployed by management down to local supervisory management and front-line staff.

☐ People, tools, equipment and other resources.

☐ Skills and competencies of staff.

Review

Measuring how we performed in executing the plan:

☐ Series of regular review meetings at each level of the business.

☐ Defined terms of reference for each meeting.

☐ Focus on identifying performance gaps against targets and understanding root causes, NOT on allocating blame!

☐ Agreement of corrective actions with due dates, to improve performance in the future.

Key inputs to the 'review' element of the cycle:

☐ Balanced set of performance measures for each level of the business.

☐ Targets and standards against which actual performance is compared.

☐ List of corrective actions agreed from previous meeting(s) to review progress and effectiveness.

☐ Summary of whether those actions have been completed and what their impact was.

Implementing the Plan-Do-Review model requires two things to be in place. The first is a clear structure, and the second is the necessary behaviours and style to engender a measurement managed organization culture. The structure is straightforward, demanding that review groups are established at all levels of the collaboration, in line with the way that measures were assigned to organizational teams or departments during its creation. In general, the further from the collaboration board, the more frequent the review meetings need to be, but the shorter time should be required. The review structure should ensure that whenever a manager is attending a review around measures using Plan-Do-Review with his manager, he or she has already conducted that same session with their direct reports. Ultimately, when the collaboration board meets, perhaps monthly, to review the overall strategic goals of the collaboration, everyone in the room has the next level of detail at their fingertips, because they have just conducted the same review process with their teams.

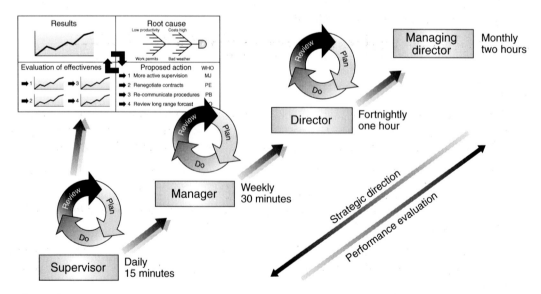

FIGURE 10.1: Plan-Do-Review cycle

Chapter 6 discussed the three important behavioural characteristics of accountability, challenge and delivering results and these depict an effective Plan-Do-Review system. What enables these behaviours to occur, however, is the clear thinking about consequences. Measures trigger the performance debate and the review meeting provides the forum. Yet the consequences for individuals of under-performance, or over-performance, will dictate whether these mechanisms lead to collaboration success. Are measures used to drive improvement, or simply the allocation of blame? Do managers have incentives to hide performance gaps or bring them into the open? The link to performance-related pay is also important here – the measures define the strategic priorities, and therefore whatever performance pay exists within the collaboration must be aligned to those performance goals.

CRITICAL TOUCH POINTS

Before leaving the topic of measures it is worth considering the other roles this underpinning system plays beyond monitoring performance for the collaboration. It is the glue that holds the collaboration together, and so measures can also drive the ongoing evolution of the model. Specifically, measures feed back into the collaboration establishment process in a number of areas:

☐ Actual performance can inform the initial thinking on the overall share goals and values of the collaboration, and help to refine them.

☐ Performance in the various parts of the collaboration can provide insight for the parent organization about whether their stated strategic needs are being met, and also whether the readiness assessment issues are being overcome or not.

☐ Measures amend and refine the integrated plan on an on-going basis. Assumptive links between actions and outcomes can be confirmed or denied, and this will drive a modification to priorities, resource investment and focus.

☐ Measures can act as the basis for organizational learning. The debate and hypotheses which flow from the Plan-Do-Review cycle can begin the process of instilling a learning organization model into the collaboration.

SUMMARY

1 The measurement model plays a critical role in supporting the intent to have a common and shared approach to operations within the collaboration, and in overcoming the differences in style, values and operating practices from the parent organizations.

2 The measurement model can be developed by following eight key guiding principles.

3 Developing the model requires five activities to be conducted: confirm the strategic measures; conduct key driver analysis; complete lower level measure deployment; conduct a bottom-up process and plan check; and finally build the data dictionary.

4 Choosing the right technology on which to build the measurement model can be done by considering delivery interface, time criticality, user manipulation, data ownership and staff access.

5   The use of Portal technology to ensure rapid implementation of the presentation interface, often drawing from multiple legacy systems, is becoming increasingly popular for such measurement models.

6   Ongoing use of measures to drive collaboration success uses the Plan-Do-Review cycle.

7   Plan-Do-Review effectiveness requires both a structure in which to operate and a clearly agreed set of consequences to engender the desired behaviours.

8   The measurement model, apart from monitoring and managing collaboration performance, can inform the goals and values, integrated plan for a learning organization and provide its foundation.

4

MANAGING IN THE
NETWORKED ECONOMY

CHAPTER 11

CREATING NETWORKED COMPANIES

A FUTURE VISION

So far this book has looked at how collaboration can augment the existing business models of organizations to help them to achieve their strategic goals faster and more effectively. We have considered how new market entry or industry dominance can be better achieved through collaborating with other powerful organizations for mutual advantage. There are many cases of how these approaches have transformed companies, and often industries, as a result. However, where could the collaboration journey take us? How far can we push the concept? Is there more to collaboration than simply improving what we know? Should the strategic perspective be drawn from a more extreme vision?

For example, consider the co-makership model, which Ford and VW use to produce their respective people carrier models, the Galaxy and the Sharan. These two cars are direct competitors in the consumer marketplace, but they are made on a shared production line that operates a common assembly track, manages a core pool of raw material suppliers and effectively charges Ford and VW 'by the hour'. In essence, two of the world's best known car manufacturers have got out of the game of making cars. In a way this is true, yet from another perspective they still have control of the facilities and define specification, quality standards and price. What does this tell us about the future place for collaboration? Or more importantly, what lessons can we draw from this in terms of the future role of organizations?

The arrival of the internet and the concept of the digital economy have opened up a new concept of how firms could, and perhaps should, be trading in this new millennium. Similar to most technology triggers, the e-business revolution brought the hype of expectation long before the reality of execution; it forgot that generating revenue, managing cost and turning cash-based profit was the capitalist constant in this technologically-enabled future. Nevertheless, the opportunity opened up by the digital economy is not going away and it has become the foundation of some of the most successful collaboration ventures that have been established.

The supply chain vision

All models of collaboration can draw from the digital economy vision. However, it is to supply chain collaborations that the concepts apply most readily and concretely. Consider the simplest possible form of this collaboration model – two organizations that have historically been in a supplier-customer relationship, operating in adjacent steps in an industry value chain. The steel producer and the car body manufacturer. The production system engineering firm and the chemical company. Or the food manufacturer and the supermarket retailer. In any of these situations, the two parties may conclude that they wish to build their futures together, and collaborate to make that a reality. A full company-to-company collaboration. Anything better achieved together, through sharing of information, joint planning and single point accountability, will be enabled. What could that look like?

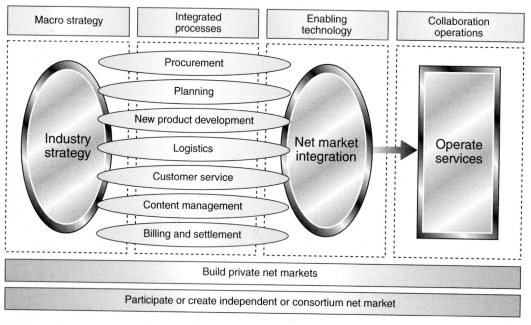

FIGURE 11.1: Supply chain collaboration in the digital economy

There are a number of possible components in this supply chain collaboration vision. We can discuss each element by using the example of a major raw material provider (the supplier) and a manufacturer (the customer), who in turn produces product for a broad marketplace.

☐ Procurement is only managed by one, common group across the collaboration. Anything related to the core business directly links the end-customer sales orders to the supplier ordering system. There is no procurement between the two organizations. Non-core procurement is managed across the group collectively, so that economies of scale through greater purchasing power can be achieved. A common e-procurement process and system is used by all staff.

☐ Planning is managed by a single group. A common information system links marketing, sales and operational plans together, and resources levels and allocation is managed as a result. The planning group sits adjacent to the collaboration board and uses the same technology, which draws data from all the transactional systems that support this group. The final operative plan on which the collaboration is run is signed off by the planning group each week, chaired by a representative from the collaboration board.

☐ Product portfolio management and new product development is a shared activity. Ideas from all parties, whether customer insight back, or product innovation forward, are managed through a single process. A joint group across the companies sits at each of the gating steps in the new product development process; no resource is wasted developing products that will ultimately be rejected by one of the parties. Common design tools are used by staff from both organizations, and ideas, drawings and concepts are stored on a single technical system.

☐ The lowest cost model for manufacturing means co-locating the operations of both organizations, and therefore the only role for logistics is outbound (facing towards the consumer). The customer firm is recognized to have far greater capability here and where the occasional management of inbound logistics is required by the supplier they support this. Increasingly though, logistics is not seen as core to either party. With the introduction of monitoring tools, for example, GPS (Global Positioning System) tracking of all orders is visible through the supply chain system, owning trucks and other transport vehicles is viewed as a burden, not an asset. Outsourcing this seems likely.

☐ Customer insight and CRM growth strategies must be managed by the customer organization in this collaboration – that insight can provide helpful guidance back up the supply chain. By introducing a full CRM system with a customer lifetime value structure and encouraging greater online engagement between the customer and their customers, complete integration from customer order through to raw material procurement can happen. This supports the growing move from make to stock, to make to order. With the whole supply chain lined up, with common information sharing across three or four value chain steps, and with the problem of stock ownership removed, this operating concept is becoming a trading reality.

☐ As the whole supply chain becomes increasingly electronic and aligned, accessing new growth markets through online NetMarkets, both public and proprietary, can easily be managed and orders fulfilled. This is simply another digital customer able to tap into this networked organization.

A broader vision for networked companies

A straightforward supply chain collaboration can be achieved, where real shareholder value is attained by all parties, with genuine single management processes and open data sharing and planning. However, with that core hub in place, the organization can start building its electronic network along many vectors.

The supplier vector – If organizations can trade in an electronic manner with suppliers, are comfortable to share with them forward visibility of customer demand, and can encourage communization of approach within the organization, the point of access to suppliers can be vastly improved. For the core business, the boundaries of organizational ownership should be based on who is most able, and who can do it for the lowest cost, not on any historic and arbitrary drawing of the line. If the supplier can part build the product for less – let them. If one of the suppliers has particular purchasing power in a supply market used by the organization, then see if your organization can piggyback on top of this. If some of the offered products or services could be directly shipped from the supplier to the customer – perhaps parts – then why should they even touch your organization's premises? Particularly if there is underpinning technology that gives visibility of that order and its fulfilment. Why own it or touch it? Just take the profit margin on it.

Of course outside the core business, the organization and a number of the largest suppliers can buy non-core spend more efficiently if the purchasing power is pooled. Everyone buys PCs – why not use the power of five times the volume to save everyone some money?

The customer vector – If all of the areas that dictate collaboration between you and strategic suppliers saves money to both parties, then that logic naturally extends up the value chain. Is there a common ordering system that will allow strategic customers to provide earlier visibility of their demand needs? Can you directly access their consumption figures to take the whole issue away from them – does ownership of fulfilment move? Or what about cross-customer benefit sharing? If there is a scarce product, yet one customer has surplus in their channel, can visibility remain right up to the point of consumption? Does it make sense to create a common trading area somewhere in the digital ether, where information can be shared about new product ideas that could benefit all? Does an insight of the end-customer bring knowledge and ideas back up the chain, which could ensure growth-driving new products for all?

The market vector – Existing customers is a very important aspect. Nevertheless, as collaboration brings not just your own company into the digital arena, but also this network of electronically linked partners through the value chain, how can this huge collective asset and resource base be taken to a broader audience group? Is there a place for a new NetMarket – either privately created with these collaborative partners or publicly sponsored? Does a potential market already exist, which would benefit from the addition of this network of companies?

The employee vector – Staff are generally the largest resource group within an organization. Yet even their structure and relationship changes as we become more connected. It is not uncommon to hear complaints in collaborations that the staff from other partner organizations are treated better than the firm's own employees. It is through this network of organizations, which is becoming a single electronic trading entity, that employee considerations emerge. Can buying power for flexible benefits like pensions, company cars or life insurance be pooled for the benefit of all? If one of the networked firms is further ahead with some of its employee benefits schemes, could this be applied to others? If one has an excellent online training and development or e-learning suite, can this become a common resource for the collaboration?

And who exactly are defined as employees? Over time, those that deliver the firm's marketplace promise are increasingly comprised of consultants, contractors, part-time staff, partners, advisors and outsourced providers. Frequently many of these 'non-employees' are working on-site, directly with employed staff. The lines are blurring. Should they be in the company directory? Should they attend team briefings? Do we want them to feel real ownership of the vision and strategy for the company? Increasingly the answer to these questions is yes, and the technology on which this network of firms is built, supports communication tools and strategy deployment mechanisms.

LESSONS LEARNED FROM THE DOT.COMS

The groups of companies who heralded the concept of networked businesses, operating in a digital economy, were the dot.coms from early 1999 to late 2000. Almost an extinct breed now, they triggered many traditional businesses to radically rethink the way they went to market and operated their businesses. Although, in general, it is the e-businesses of the traditional firms that have won over the young start-ups, the latter did leave behind an innovative business model that can move us further towards this networked vision.

In the consumer marketplace, the genuine dot.coms are worth considering further. For the business-to-business environment the online exchanges and auctions, around 5000 of them so far, attempted to achieve a similar goal. In addition, some organizations tried to play both fields, for example, eBay's venture into its business exchange service. What was the fundamental business model of these innovative, if often unsuccessful, organizations?

For most of the consumer dot.coms the proposition was broadly the same. Own nothing. Create a mass customer base fast by using the internet and off-line advertising as the route into the consumer market, and then offer a product, service and price mix that cannot be found elsewhere. Use collaborative partners to fulfil, and in most cases run, practically all of the operational processes. For Expedia.com, the consumer offer was visibility of all travel options and immediate reservations, which topped $1 trillion last year. For eBay.com, the unique factor was the ability to trade interesting products, about 450,000 per day to be precise, in a model that moved away from 'fixed price commerce'. Uniquely eBay.com was profitable from its first month of trading. And lastminute.com provided access to all forms of presents, entertainment and holidays for those poor at planning, and often at knock-down prices.

Interestingly, almost no dot.coms tried to bring new products to the marketplace. The almost universal proposition was based around what mix could be bought from one location, the ease in which it could be bought, and the price competitiveness of those products. At this time most traditional businesses were still worrying about product quality and product development, while the dot.coms stole a march by delivering lifestyle access to customers' homes. Running warehouses, managing stock, operating billing systems, even supporting the dot.com websites, were assigned to organizations competent in those areas. Few of the dot.coms could see any sustainable value or differentiation in these areas. Why take on operational pain when someone else can do it for you? They can manage the risk and challenge of being on the delivery end of a clearly structured service level agreement. Many of the dot.coms who succeeded, filed accounts showing turnover of hundreds and sometimes billions of dollars, from organizations reporting staff levels of less than 100.

The online exchanges operated in a very similar way. Typically created by groups of organizations in the industry, the online exchanges tended to propose a similar vision:

- ☐ Improve efficiency across an industry supply chain.
- ☐ Provide access to new markets.
- ☐ Reduce third-party costs.
- ☐ Provide improved business intelligence.
- ☐ Share investment in technology.
- ☐ Increase speed to market for new products.
- ☐ Agree standards for e-business.

In general terms, the exchanges have suffered the same fate as many of the dot.coms. Roughly half have already gone out of business, and only 15 per cent have the ability to do proper end-to-end transactions. However, some have succeeded, with exchanges in retail, chemicals and automotives all breaking the $100 million mark in their first six months. The common factor they had with the dot.coms is very few staff employed by the exchange, yet in many cases offering the full delivery capability of a whole industry value chain.

By considering the business models of the dot.coms and exchanges, and by balancing this innovation with the challenge of achieving financial viability, what lessons can be learned for potential end-game collaborations which increasingly rely on the enabling technology of the digital economy?

☐ Recognize the critical assets or resources that the organization must own if it is to achieve its strategic goals. Challenge historical views about what the organization really needs to hold on to, versus what could be delivered through collaborative relationships.

☐ Underpin any collaborative relationship, particularly a proposition-based collaboration, with a clear business model that identifies the sources of revenue and the real drivers of cost.

☐ Consider how technology can enable collaborative relationships to work across a broad scope of activities – from joint product development through to cross-company integrated planning. Building or piggybacking a trading infrastructure for this, with potentially new partners coming in and out of that network based on specific projects or customers, provides the tool to achieve the networked goal.

☐ Take the 'blank sheet of paper' approach. If there were no legacy issues to address, in the same way that exchanges and dot.coms can start from scratch, how would a collaboration work ideally?

NECESSARY PRECURSORS

The extreme position is to create a truly networked organization that takes the concept of collaboration to its end-state. Your organization would prefer to execute no activities if that could be achieved. You wish to dominate a market area by simply bringing together the capability of collaborative partners who collectively can deliver your organization's strategy. You are starting from the point of having an existing organization that broadly does all of the activities required to deliver the marketplace promise. Moving to become a networked organization is a vast step. What precursors need to be in place to make such a move happen? There are five critical factors that need to be fully understood and in place before the journey can start: knowing what is core, understanding the relationship model, executing transitions effectively, customer interface clarity and managing corporate risk.

1 Knowing what is core

The traditional debate about core and non-core has been the focus for executives to decide what should or should not be outsourced. In doing this, the underlying assumption was that the need for strategic control and direct ownership of those activities were synonymous. With the emergence of collaborative models, and indeed a fuller understanding of the entire relationship continuum, this base assumption is invalid. However, the critical question of 'Where do I need to keep strategic control?' is still pertinent. Before the route to a more networked organization can begin, firms must comprehend where they need to retain strategic control and where they simply require acceptable operational performance. Whether those strategic control areas, or even the operational ones, should be kept in-house, is addressed by understanding the relationship continuum. Assess whether there is an organization in the market who could operate in the appropriate relationship model and deliver the area in question more efficiently or effectively than the in-house team.

2 Understanding the relationship model

Business-to-business relationships operate along a continuum. Starting from 'spot' suppliers right the way through to a full joint venture, passing standard supplier relationships, outsourcing and partnerships along the way, the key point is that there are different models that dictate different ways of operating. The type of contract, the degree of information sharing and the importance of cultural fit will differ depending on the model of relationship. Having an extensive network does not necessitate moving everything to a collaborative model. Nevertheless, collaborations will form the core of that model because this relationship structure should govern all strategic elements of the business. However, the tools and infrastructure put in place for collaborations can be leveraged for other forms of relationships. Clarifying these boundaries is a critical precursor.

Executing transitions effectively

Highly developed networks tend to involve a high degree of asset movement. These assets may be buildings, production facilities, stock, patents or people. Networked organizations are interested in managing outcomes, not the activities to deliver them. Managing the resource base should sit with whoever is best able to do it. Therefore, being able to manage transition processes is crucial, particularly when this involves people, TUPE rules (the legal processes that protect employment rights when a company is acquired), relocation policies and, most importantly, managing morale through a period of uncertainty.

Customer interface clarity

Managing the customer interface in networked businesses is a little like applying the concept of Portal technology. With a Portal, all sorts of legacy systems, transactional systems, manual inputs and even spreadsheets are invisibly pulled together to deliver exactly what the information users want. This presentation tool looks great, is highly branded, tailored, flexible and responsive. Networked organizations need to be at this standard. Although the task of managing multiple organizations 'behind the scenes,' can become so all-encompassing that no one steps into the customers' shoes to make sure the delivery still looks joined up from their perspective. No matter who executes activities, the view to the customer needs to be one of seamless integration.

Managing corporate risk

When all the processes required to deliver the firm's product and services are owned by the organization, corporate focus tends to be operational risk management. As the networked world emerges, the focus moves towards managing outputs, not activities. This focus is reflected in the understanding and management of risk. Organizations need to manage strategic risks, not operational ones, in a manner that ensures the countervailing forces of risk control and trust building do not create a conflict. Otherwise, the firm could be left in the middle ground where, unable to make a true collaboration work, it has not given itself a low-cost route out either.

CRITICAL CONSIDERATIONS

Collaboration is the core relationship model for organizations that wish to access the digital economy opportunity. As the collaborative technology platform is built and the door opens for other relationship models, there are three critical considerations that firms must understand and master to succeed in this new world. Firstly, organizations need to recognize that only two core competencies truly matter – the ability to master strategy and the ability to manage third-party relationships. All other competencies, while having their place in the organizations development, can be transient. Secondly, today's choice along the relationship continuum may not be the same for all time. Effective collaborative relationships could grow and indicate that a merger is the right way to progress. Equally, what is deemed strategic now may be less so in two or three years' time, and the relationship may need to regress. And thirdly, the bigger game. Networking organizations involves big choices. Which exchange to join? By collaborating with one supplier a clear message is sent to another. When organizations make their choices of who to align with, they also turn trading relationships away. All of this happens within an environment where every industry sector is consolidating – not just nationally, but globally – and the boundaries between industry sectors are blurring. How do you manage this game of industry roulette?

The three big issues

Chapters 12–14 consider each of the three critical considerations in more detail. Between them they represent some of the most challenging questions that chief executives are grappling with today. Excellence in operational management, involving hundreds of daily decisions, is giving way to strategic positioning, where one or two crucial choices define success or failure for the whole corporation.

SUMMARY

1 This book has focused so far on how collaboration approaches can augment existing business models. However, the same tools can apply to a new business model.

2 The arrival of the digital economy lays the technology foundation to permit organizations to genuinely operate as networked organizations.

3 Networked businesses, such as those operating full supply chain collaboration, can collaborate on all fronts, including sales, marketing, new product development, joint planning, logistics and new market entry.

4 Evolving networked businesses is typically along four key vectors: supplier, customer, market and employee.

5 Creating a networked business demands five precursors to be in place:

   ☐ Understanding what is core to the businesses and, therefore, where strategic control needs to be maintained.

   ☐ Understanding each relationship model that can be used within the networked world.

   ☐ Managing large-scale transitions well – whether people, assets or other resources.

☐ Clarifying how changes in activity execution will remain invisible to the seamless delivery of customer service.

☐ Recognizing that risk will move away from a process focused on operational excellence, to one driven by strategic agenda items.

6 Operating firms in the networked economy will require excellence in three critical areas:

☐ The ability to develop strategy and to manage partners.

☐ The ability to develop relationships up and down the continuum as the strategy dictates.

☐ Understanding how to play at the industry table and recognizing the ramifications of the choices of who to network with, and who to walk away from.

CHAPTER 12

STRATEGY AND PARTNER MANAGEMENT

WHY STRATEGY AND PARTNER?

If we return to the dot.com examples, all of these organizations had two things in common. A clear view on the unique proposition they could take to the marketplace – they had a strategy – and focus on managing a variety of business partners in order to make that strategy become a reality. Although some proved themselves poor in both of these areas, they were the two critical competencies needed to be successful. And so it is for those organizations moving closer and closer towards becoming networked businesses – something only remains under their direct control if they can do it better or cheaper than an external party.

As previously stated, collaboration is not the only relationship model to deliver third-party execution of the strategy for networked organizations. However, it is the dominant model for all areas of strategic significance. Chapter 13 considers the different types of relationship model in much greater detail, and where collaboration fits into this framework. Returning to the issue of strategy, while most organizations would claim to have a strategy, the corporate world's success rate is not high. The well-publicized findings of Kaplan and Norton confirms this[1]:

- ☐ 90 per cent of companies fail to execute the strategy they set themselves.
- ☐ 85 per cent of executives spend less than one hour per month discussing strategy.
- ☐ 60 per cent of companies do not link budgets to strategy.
- ☐ Only 25 per cent of managers have incentives linked to strategy.
- ☐ Less than 5 per cent of the workforce understand the strategy.

Networked organizations need to build their success upon strategy – but how does one overcome this apparent gap in capability and understanding?

136

[1] The Balanced Scorecard was first mentioned in the Harvard Business Review article 'Putting the Balanced Scorecard to Work' by R S Kaplan and D P Norton in the September–October 1993 edition.

BUILDING EFFECTIVE STRATEGIES

There are many definitions of what a strategy is and what it does. Some definitions draw on the historic position of military strategy, others talk about strategy as the manner in which decisions are made. For the purposes of networked organizations, strategy will be defined in the following way:

> Strategy is the creative process that aids resource allocation decisions . . .

> . . . to give the company an advantage over its competitors . . .

> . . . both now and in the future . . .

> . . . allowing the firm to earn returns on capital in excess of its cost of capital.

It is important, when discussing strategy, to return to the question of scope. What are we considering when we talk about strategy? Is it the corporate whole, a specific business unit or a functional or process area? For General Electric, corporate strategy is a broad portfolio game, closer to an investment bank than to an operational company. With diverse businesses in different markets, it is unlikely that a networked company model can develop across them. For most organizations, the strategy is most critical at the business unit level – here customer sets, market drivers and direct competitors are contemplated. If we go one level below this, to functional or process strategies, by their very definition they need to have developed from a higher level strategy and are, therefore, closer to operational strategies than true business strategies.

It is not just the level of the strategy that we need to be clear upon – within what geographical scope are we developing this approach? Does it cover all customer industry areas? Once the answers to these questions are clear, we are in a position to develop the strategy to create our delivery capability.

The strategy landscape

Organizations should consider three specific issues when building a strategy:

1   Identify an appropriate set of objectives.

2   Identify where the organization will and will not compete – selecting the battlefields.

3   Align capabilities to ensure successful competition and achievement of objectives.

There are a number of contributing factors to study as inputs to the thought process. Together this set of factors describes the landscape upon which business strategies can be developed.

Identifying appropriate objectives

Gaining consensus for a set of appropriate strategic objectives requires a balance to be found between what we would like to do (stakeholder aspirations), what is available to do (environmental attractiveness) and what we are able to do (resource availability). Each of these three areas can be analyzed in its own right, but the development of a final set of objectives is inevitably an iterative process.

Stakeholder aspirations – Although stakeholder balance is an important factor, the demands from lenders and the expectations of shareholders will typically have the strongest influence on what are, or are not, appropriate strategic objectives. Lender and shareholder expectations will combine an element of their appetite with risk, and their perspectives on attractive

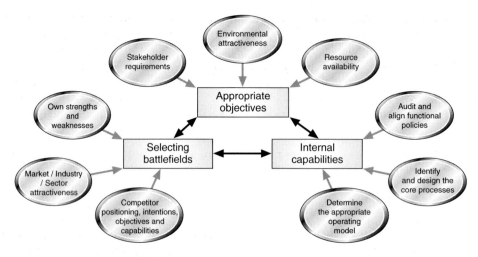

FIGURE 12.1: The strategy landscape

market opportunities and how much they are prepared to trade short-term profit for longer term return. Recognize that, in almost all cases, both lenders and shareholders will play a portfolio game; investing in your organization as part of a broader investment strategy, playing within a higher level risk/return equation.

The other major stakeholders are always the executives of the organization themselves and, in particular, the personal ambitions of the chief executive officer. Governance theory suggests that strategy should be independent of the officers who hold post, but almost every major success or failure story in corporate history suggests that this is not the case.

Finally, there are other stakeholders to consider – employees and managers, government, the environment and, in some instances, regulatory bodies. For some, these stakeholder groups contribute to the aspiration of the business, for others they provide constraints within which the strategic objectives must be developed. In all situations, there will be conflict between the different stakeholder groups. The role of the executive team is to create a path which is acceptable to all and offers the best future to the organization.

Environmental attractiveness – Later battlefields are selected on which to marshal corporate resources, but first the wars we wish to fight need to be picked. At a macro-economic level, this is mostly an analytical review of potential industries or markets in which to play, their growth rates, our competitive position and, normally, our starting point. What level of share do we already have? Environmental attractiveness is simply one data point in the debate of strategic objectives. It tells us where the most exciting and profitable places to trade are, yet it provides little insight about whether we are able to succeed, or indeed what it would take, to dominate those trading arenas.

Evaluating relative competitive position is important here and cannot be considered as a static model. In Chapter 5, where competitive collaborations were discussed, the challenge of not only reviewing the current competitive arena, but running scenarios to predict competitor reactions and take proactive steps, needs to be built into the evaluation. At the end of this step we should know where we would ideally want to play.

Resource availability – Resource availability is the most common reason that nine out of ten firms do not achieve their strategy. It is too easy to be carried away with what is possible, and forget what the organization is able to do. Resources can cover a broad spectrum – financial muscle, skills, core competencies, and ability to be innovative. Nonetheless, broadly it comes down to financial strength. Skills, capabilities, even patents and IPR can all be bought, if a firm has sufficient investment funds. The capability to manage partners is critical in this model; if we buy the competence we need, but do not have the skills to manage and harness it, it is all for nothing. What options are possible, given the resources of the organization? Building a new plant in China to access a profitable, growing market may be what our environmental review suggests – but if our cash position does not permit this, it is a pointless conversation.

At the end of this step we understand what we want to achieve – what our strategic ambitions are – but we do not know how to turn them into reality.

Selecting battlefields

From our objectives we know where we wish to win and now we need a battle plan to turn that into reality. A route map is needed. Achievement in this area is about knowing ourselves (strengths and weakness), knowing our foe (competitor position) and knowing our battles (market attractiveness). The battlegrounds are chosen last – they are self-selecting, depending on our views of the relative competitive position between our organization and the competitors who could prevent us achieving our stated strategic objectives.

Strengths and weakness – Knowing, in a genuinely objective manner, the relative strengths and weaknesses of your own organization is pivotal to develop effective strategy. It is also a useful process to inform the organization where collaborative relationships may be appropriate. However, it carries real challenges. Commonly the relative performance of different parts of the business is based heavily on perception. Take functional strengths as an example. Is your finance function, or sales or marketing better or worse than the competition? Comparing the functions internally gives no insight, because they are incomparable. Often the view of performance internally focuses on a few key personalities, not on the overall resource and capability of the function. And finally, who really knows how good the competitors are?

Comparing marketplace issues is simpler. For example, product or service strengths and weaknesses, geographical position and coverage, channel control and dominance. More facts can be brought to bear. For the more internally-focused areas, this benchmarking assessment can be helpful to bring about that objective baseline.

Competitor position – We need to understand three things about our competitors:

1 Where are they currently positioned (in terms of their share of markets, products and geographies)?

2 What are their intentions (i.e. where are they focusing their resources going forward)?

3 What are their capabilities to achieve this (in terms of financial resources, skills, capabilities and infrastructure)?

This evaluation is most useful if you use the same framework as you have to assess your own organization's strengths and weaknesses. The outcome of the exercise can illustrate relative competitive positions along each of the appropriate dimensions for all potential players in the competitive game.

Market attractiveness – Market attractiveness is about making specific choices. Do we extend the product range in the UK, or take the existing product offer to Italy? Is it easier to add 5 per cent to our dominant market share in the United States, or begin an organic start up in

Korea, where nobody is operating? Should we divest our interests in Eastern Europe and use these savings to grow South America? Stated priorities are known, and so is the balance expected by our stakeholders in short and long-term returns. Fundamentally, market attractiveness is about 'bang for your buck'. It is necessary to be clear on two facts:

1 How much opportunity is there in the particular market segment (defined by customer, product or geography)?

2 What is our likelihood of accessing that opportunity (relative competitive position)?

Pulling these factors together provides a clear marketplace strategy – we have picked our battlefields and we know what we must do to win on them.

Aligning capabilities

Here we truly begin to consider the move towards networked-based businesses. We know what we are trying to achieve, and we know what we must do to find success. It is essential to make sure that the resources are in place, capable and focused to deliver. There are three factors to discuss – business control (functional policies), process capability (core process design) and an appropriate *modus operandi* (operating model).

Functional policies – Often missed out from the strategic planning process, ensuring that appropriate controls are in place is necessary for the strategy to be achieved. This approach is even more significant when companies increasingly deliver their goals through third-party relationships, and as they bring those third parties, particularly lower down the relationship continuum, into their digital network. What are the third parties authorized to do? What levels of information in each of the functional areas should be shared? How do we ensure that common standards are used for data and information? What accounting policies will we use and how does this impact on our reported performance? All issues of authority levels, standards and policy need to be defined as part of the strategy, then control can be achieved regardless of who is executing the activities.

Core process design – Put simply, the strategy stage must deliver a process strategy. Firstly, what are the business processes, and secondly, what do each of them have to achieve if the strategic objectives are to be fulfilled? Chapter 2, when considering the approach to supply chain collaboration, focused on the fact that this model of collaboration provides a design to move business process execution to another organization to be executed. If we are to live in a networked world, where the execution can be moved outside our own organization's borders, there must be absolute clarity on what that process does and what it delivers into the overall strategy. The means to achieve this, looking at objective deployment to business process, is covered in Chapter 2, but it is important to understand where and how it fits into the broader strategic landscape.

Operating model – Finally, how does it all hang together? What is the organizational strategy through which our objectives can be achieved? We have considered the operating model appropriate to each of the four models of collaboration, but to ensure these collaborations are truly successful, we need to have a clear view of the operating model of our own organization. This will need to cover topics, such as:

☐ Structure.

☐ Systems.

☐ Skills.

☐ Management style.

☐ Staff.

☐ Culture and values.

When studying the operating model, the implications and principles of networked companies also need to be considered. How does the model of the extended organization show itself in daily operation? How important are consistent values to those that deliver the marketplace promise of the organization, regardless of which firm employs these people? To what should these staff feel a sense of belonging and pride? What is the right model of management in an extended organization? Is it the same in all areas? What systems do we need in order to enable this seamless delivery into the marketplace – while managing an end-to-end value chain across channels and organizations in the most efficient and effective way?

THE STRATEGIC OUTCOME

For the strategy to be effective as a framework by which a firm can manage specific collaboration relationships and, more broadly, operate a networked business, it needs to contain five elements:

1 A broad differentiation strategy.

2 A market strategy.

3 A process strategy.

4 An organizational strategy.

5 A set of key performance metrics (KPMs) that monitor all of the above.

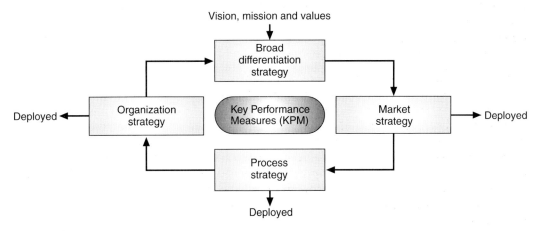

FIGURE 12.2: Strategic management framework

Each organization that is part of this business network needs to clearly understand which of the three deployed strategies they contribute to, and how. For collaborative relationships, Chapter 8 discussed how shared goals and values are created, which specifically and explicitly support this strategic framework. Chapter 9 covered the way that an integrated plan is produced, which again feeds into this model. However, how do we manage the organizations that form part of our networked business? If we are at the extreme of the model, and our only function is to achieve strategy by managing other organizations – what are the tools and approaches we use to do that? How is partner management directed.

PARTNER MANAGEMENT

Chapter 13 focuses on how relationships evolve, and in particular on three areas relating to the collaborative model. The first is when relationships lower down the continuum should move into a collaborative model, and how to recognize this; the second is when an existing collaborative model is no longer appropriate and either needs to be exited or turned into a lower form of relationship; and the third is where a collaborative relationship becomes so strategic that it needs to move to the final step on the relationship continuum – an acquisition or merger.

For networked organizations, where partners are managed on any step of the relationship continuum, there are three essential elements to put in place:

1 The relationship should begin with the partner placed at the **appropriate** step on the relationship continuum.

2 There needs to be a clear **process** to manage partner's performance and relationship.

3 The organization needs to have the **structure and capability** to execute that process effectively.

Together, these three elements allow effective management of all parties in the network – to work together in an appropriate manner and to achieve the stated strategic objectives of the organization.

Pick the right start point

To truly capitalize on the opportunities presented by the digital economy and to operate our organization as a genuinely networked corporation, even a supplier who we buy from based on spot market price, should be part of this technology-linking web. The supplier may be a registered supplier on the auction part of our open infrastructure, where they have the obligation to keep their product and service range up to date, with the latest prices. However, they can still form part of this extended network, informed each time there is an online auction where one of the products or service they have registered goes out to tender. It is crucial though, that being part of our network does not confuse the type of relationship we should be having with that firm.

All relationships between organizations exist along a continuum – for simplicity we have chosen a model that has five points (Table 12.1). As a continuum, any of these elements could be broken into more refined classifications. A merger, for example, could include equity investment, joint venture and acquisition as three sub-categories.

Choosing the model from which to begin the relationship is governed by two factors:

1 How strategically important are the products or services upon which the relationship is based?

2 What is the level of trust or risk involved in the relationship?

Relationship potential is not a factor, because we will later have a process to evolve relationships up and down the continuum.

Strategic importance is relatively easy to assess, and is likely to be governed by factors such as value, criticality, core versus non-core and customer impact. This could lead us to decide that our relationship with a particular organization should be one of collaboration, or at least

DISTINCTIVE CHARACTERISTICS	SPOT	BUYER SUPPLIER	PREFERRED SUPPLIER	COLLABORATE	MERGER
RELATIONSHIP MANAGEMENT	Sales/Purchasing	Sales/Purchasing	Key account manager and lead buyer	Cross-functional team	Internal
TYPICAL CONTRACT TERM	None	None to Quarterly	Quarterly to Annual	Annual to Multi-year	Ongoing
TYPE OF PRODUCT/ SERVICE	Commodity	Transaction-based	Major spend categories	Strategic	Strategic
IMPORTANCE OF CULTURAL FIT	Low	Low	Medium	High	High
BUYING CRITERIA	Price	Price and quality	Total cost, quality and delivery	Value	N/A

TABLE 12.1: Relationship continuum

preferred supplier – either on the supply side or the buy side. However, what of the issue of trust and risk?

Trust relates to the observations of behaviour, if there is an existing relationship. Some organizations have a mature corporate style to deal with third-party partners – others do not. Even if an organization appears to be an ideal fit in all other regards, without that level of mutual maturity, anything other than a basic relationship will not succeed.

Risk is a more quantifiable issue, and there are two areas to be considered. Firstly, internal risk. For example, if the partner is the sole provider of a critical component of your core process, this fundamental supply-demand inequality could drive undesired behaviours and this could lead to an alternative relationship approach being more appropriate. Secondly, market or competitive risk. If an ideal preferred supplier for your organization is already collaborating with your fiercest competitor, will you ever achieve the level of focus and resource priority from them that you require?

Balancing strategic desire with the constraints of risk and fit, should allow the correct placement of each organization you wish to operate with, in a networked manner. It may also highlight gaps along the continuum, which demand new partners to be found.

Define a clear process

Partner management does not necessitate a difficult process – but it does require one that is mutually agreed and understood by all parties. It is easier if this process is the same for all of the relationship models, and then a set of tools and terminology can be commonly applied. The way that each step is applied, and the amount of effort applied to it will be different for each of the types of relationship. There are six steps for a partner management process.

1 Agree mutual expectations – Firstly and most importantly, there needs to be a common view about which relationship model is used. If the supplier wishes to be in a collaborative relationship, but your intentions are for a simple preferred supplier model, make that explicit and known upfront. The other important factors to agree at this point are the scope of the relationship (which products and services), the method of relationship management (what level of face-to-face time should they be expecting, and with whom, versus 'automated' interactions), where respective roles and responsibilities lie, the level of information sharing and joint planning expected, and the level of resource effort expected from both parties.

2 Define performance measures – Expectations become tangible when translated into specific performance measures. Chapter 10 covered the critical importance of the measurement model for the operation of a collaboration relationship, but measures are important for all other models. They define targets and they specify focus. For a spot relationship in a commodity area, the only relevant measure might be unit price. If that is the case, make that mutual expectation known and when the review process takes place, price should be the only agenda item.

3 Agree the relationship plan – A plan is needed to monitor that the relationship is operating as desired. This plan may specify which parts of the open technology infrastructure the partner has access to, and how they interact with it. It may set in place the timings and agenda for review meetings. It may include when and how common reporting is distributed. It will certainly define the execution activities for the scope of work around which the relationship is based. Contract signing will form part of the planning step with expectations and measures already outlined. An appropriate contract, representative of the level of relationship sought, can be put in place.

4 Execute against the plan – Operational delivery of the agreed tasks of work. In this step, the role of the partner manager is limited to merely ensure that no material issues occur, either from the partner or the organization's perspective, that require action in advance of planned review meetings. The role, therefore, is simply a reactive one.

5 Review performance – Contract, expectations and measures form the basis for the review process. We have previously discussed that this will be through a board structure that has a clear review and governance role for a collaboration. Moving back along the relationship continuum, the frequency and scope of the review session diminishes. For spot suppliers, review may take the form of electronic feedback against customer expectation, rather than any face-to-face discussion. The principles of the Plan-Do-Review cycle will apply as much to the partner management process as it does to the collaboration performance management model.

6 Refine and learn – Review drives learning. This may involve reconsidering the scope, expectations, contractual form, method of communication, or a host of other areas. This learning loop is also a critical feed into the topic of Chapter 13 – the evolution of the relationship model.

Organize for success

The starting point is known, there is a process to manage from there – the final stage is to ensure that the organization is equipped to manage that process effectively. A structure to deal with the process and the right skill sets in-house to do so are required.

Structure is the most straightforward area to address. In a networked economy, working with and managing third-party relationships is paramount and there needs to be a group of dedicated individuals who do this. Historically, the places where such skills normally lie are with senior buyers from procurement, and key account managers in sales. Other pockets of skills may exist where outsourced functions, such as IT, payroll or general support, have had to be managed internally. The core group of individuals need to manage the process – both internally and externally – and explain to all parties how their actions support that process.

Increasingly this group, and the group that develops strategy, are becoming synonymous. Their role, after all, is to monitor and manage the execution of strategy through their own resources, and through those belonging to other organizations. This core group also often needs the ability to create the technical architecture in order to make the network an operational reality. As an overall group, analytical skills, strategic thinking capability, relationship management and trust building, and a strong performance management focus are the prerequisites for success.

SUMMARY

1 Networked organizations need to build competence in two critical areas: the development and deployment of strategy, and the management of partners within the network.

2 For the purposes of a networked business, we define strategy as the creative process, which aids resource allocation decisions in order to give the company an advantage over its competitors, both now and in the future. This allows the firm to earn returns on capital in excess of its cost of capital.

3 Historically, nine out of ten firms fail to achieve their stated strategic goals, which is why strategy deployment is as important as strategy development.

4 Strategy development requires organizations to:

☐ Identify an appropriate set of objectives.

☐ Identify where the organization will compete – selecting the battlefields.

☐ Align capabilities to ensure successful competition and achievement of objectives.

5 The output of the strategy process contains a differentiation strategy, a market strategy, a process strategy, an organizational strategy and a set of key performance measures, around which progress can be monitored.

6 The key performance measures are the direct feed into the measures model for a collaboration.

7 Managing partners within the network starts with a clear understanding of which relationship model is appropriate. While collaborative relationships form the core of a networked business, all other relationship models can and should be part of the digital infrastructure for operation management.

8 Managing partners necessitates a common process. This includes setting expectation, defining performance measures, agreeing a plan, executing against that plan, reviewing performance and then refining and learning.

9 Firms need to organize themselves to successfully manage these networked partners, focusing both on structure and skills.

CHAPTER 13

RELATIONSHIP EVOLUTION

BASE ASSUMPTIONS

The world is in a constant state of change. The author, Charles Handy's view is often quoted about organizations. He believes that if organizations do not completely reinvent themselves every five years they will not succeed. Business pundits enjoyed reviewing the great companies described in the book *In Search of Excellence*[1] on its ten-year anniversary of publication, and expounding on the fact that so many of these so-called role models were now floundering, if not out of business. So did Tom Peters get the book wrong? Did he pick companies that were not models of excellence? Of course not. All that happened was that time for two of Handy's complete reinventions had passed, but some of these organizations had not followed his guidance. If organizations themselves need to change, so do the relationships they hold with third parties. A critical collaborative partner today may be irrelevant in five years, or indeed, more fundamental than large parts of the current organization.

A process to manage relationship evolution is crucial. For this, some base elements need to be in place, which we have already covered in this book:

☐ A model which describes the relationship continuum for our own organization, and which clearly names and defines the characteristics of each of the steps along that continuum.

☐ A clearly articulated business strategy, which has been translated into deployable strands for market, process and organization.

☐ A partner management process, which allows setting of expectation and operating and reviewing the performance of each relationship.

☐ An internal organizational unit accountable for managing third-party assets.

☐ The technology infrastructure, which allows us to operate a networked organization, clearly defining how organizations at each step along the relationship continuum operate within this interconnected world.

146

[1] Tom Peters, *In Search of Excellence*, Advanced Management Reports, 1985.

With these building blocks in place, we need to effectively understand how to identify whether a planned relationship is operating at the jointly agreed point along the relationship continuum. We may have decided that a particular partner sits at the preferred supplier relationship model. This is an aspiration. Does it reflect day-to-day reality? Are they performing to that standard? To answer these questions, a way to evaluate partner 'outcome', as opposed to partner aspiration, is needed. How can we categorize our third-party relationships based on actual contribution?

The buy-sell hierarchy

Reviewing real outcomes involves placing a business-to-business relationship on the buy-sell hierarchy. The hierarchy defines what the relationship actually does for us. It is not a strategic model, nor a definition of characteristics or aspirations. It simply tries to define reality. What level of contribution does a trading relationship make? The hierarchy has five levels (Figure 13.1).

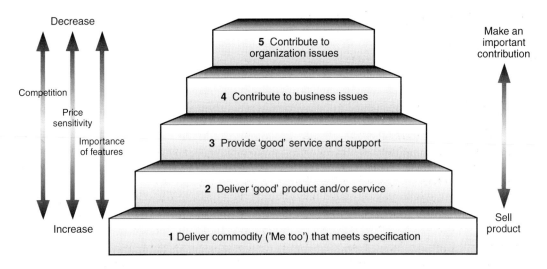

FIGURE 13.1: The buy-sell hierarchy

As the steps of the hierarchy are crossed, the degree of open competition diminishes, the role of unit selling price becomes less and less relevant, and the importance of the features of the product or service exchanged becomes peripheral to the core contribution that the relationship provides to the strategic aims of the organization. In broad terms, each of the steps in the buy-sell hierarchy match a marker along the relationship continuum. For example, delivering commodities is characterized by a spot supplier relationship. Collaboration does more than provide excellent service and support – it impacts on the business issues of the parent organizations. As we move from business issue contribution to impacting upon the organizational development of the founding organization, the question of acquisition is raised. Let's consider each of the steps along the route.

Step 1 Deliver commodities – The first distinction to make when defining commodities, is that there is no definition other than in the eyes of the customer. Money is the greatest commodity on the planet. A dollar bill is worth a dollar. Yet some of the biggest organizations on the planet have managed to persuade large elements of the consumer marketplace that in fact, money is not a commodity. For some reason, the dollars from an exclusive private bank seem to be worth more than a dollar from an ordinary high street provider. Same currency. Same commodity. Visible rates of interest. Even the same credit rating. However, in the eyes of the customer, there is a difference – and that is all that matters.

The challenge for businesses is frequently the opposite. Suppliers are desperate to convince you that their product is differentiated from that of their competition. Nevertheless, if that message is not forceful enough to create a perception gap in the eyes of the customer, it is of no value. Commodity relationships are evidenced by:

☐ The customer is able to define the standard they require.

☐ There is no commercial value to the customer in the standard being exceeded.

☐ Availability and price are the only two areas where one supplier can outperform another.

PCs are a good example of a supply market, which, for many companies, has moved into the commodity layer. The firm has set its PC standard in terms of operating memory, software set up, processing speed and so on. If you want to exceed the standard that is fine – but the standard is the basis for the network infrastructure and anything more than that does not save costs. If the firm decides it wishes to order 400 new PCs, all that matters is that you can meet the standard, can deliver them when they are required, and that your price is the lowest. End of story. Commodity relationships are easy to observe – they are governed by the rule of 'buy cheap'.

Step 2 Deliver 'good' products and service – The next level in the hierarchy is still entirely focused on the product or service exchanged at the organizational interface. The difference between this model and that of commodity relationships is there are things in the eyes of the customer that are worth paying more for. There is an ability to differentiate. For a product-based relationship, this is often about features and functions. Your product can physically do more things, some of which have value to the customer. The phone system you install has routing facilities and group pick up, which the customer perceives will improve staff efficiency.

For a service-based relationship, this differentiation may be around either setting commitments or extending the scope of the service. The overnight courier service that guarantees delivery by 10.00 a.m. The car hire company that will collect the car from your office, rather than requiring you to return it. These 'bells and whistles' are the areas where you can set yourself apart from competitors in the same field, and be noticed by the customer as an innovator. These additional elements to the product or service mix increase the value to the customer organization, and allow for a higher level relationship to emerge.

Two things demonstrate the emergence of this relationship model – either the customer is prepared to pay more for apparently the 'same' product or service, or the customer continually uses a particular partner at the same price, because these added features make the purchase of higher value. Step 2 relationships tend to be relatively transient. Either the 'bells and whistles' can be relatively easily replicated by competitors, and the product or service returns to a commodity in the eyes of the customer or, alternatively, the value gap is further enhanced by moving up to Step 3 in the buy-sell hierarchy.

Step 3 Provide 'good' service and support – In moving to Step 3, a bridge is crossed in terms of the relationship model. We are no longer only in the game of selling the products and services we offer. We are now ensuring that they are fit for purpose on an ongoing basis. Return to the simple example of the new phone system. That is a product sale. However, we could, as part of the relationship, train users how to use the function, monitor, through remote technology, the up time of the system, and automatically come and repair it if anything breaks down. If we monitor usage and recommend increased capacity when it is needed, we are no longer in the business of selling telephone systems, we are the firm's telephony system provider. An ongoing model. A mutually dependent relationship. Although not solving any great business dilemma – unless perhaps operating call centres is the firm's core business – we have moved to a relationship model where a small part of the daily operations of the customers depends on a continuous relationship with the provider.

Service, support or both, categorize this level of relationship. The supplying firm is either ensuring that something which the customer has purchased is proactively maintained, or that the mechanism for reactive response to failure exists. Most non-strategic outsourced relationships fit into this step on the buy-sell hierarchy. A strategic goal of the organization is not delivered through the outsourced relationship, but part of the operation is either serviced or supported by the third-party organization.

Step 4 Contribute to business issues – Now we enter the world of collaboration. By definition, a collaborative relationship must contribute to assist the parent organization to address its core business issues. For a collaborative relationship to be an appropriate model, the focus of its existence must be strategic. Business issues are at the core and this can be observed by looking for some obvious traits:

☐ Both parties understand the business problems and objectives of the other party's organization, as well as their own.

☐ Recommendations are focused on solutions, rather than a product or service mix. While the solution will undoubtedly contain elements of the firm's products and services, it is the outcome which is sold, not the component inputs.

☐ Ideas generated to resolve problems focus on the long-term impact on profitability, not just short-term, day-to-day operational needs.

☐ Price is rarely discussed in the relationship. The focus is on revenue generation, cost reduction or organizational effectiveness. It is about growing the size of the profit pie that can be shared, not squabbling over the split of the existing pie.

Contribution at this level is characterized by the third party running part of the customer's business, not executing agreed actions. The third party takes the required strategic outcomes and puts in place the elements of the solution necessary to achieve them.

Step 5 Contribute to organizational issues – At the top of the buy-sell hierarchy there is a change in direction of the source of strategic insight. At Step 4, the collaborative partner enables the parent organization to deliver its business strategy more effectively or efficiently than it could on its own. Stepping up a level, the knowledge, insight and capability of that partner, usually in a particular area, has become greater than that of the parent organization providing direction. Suddenly, the basis to inform strategic direction is better placed with the partner rather than the customer. This can take many forms, but examples could include:

☐ The ability to define the product portfolio strategy, which will achieve success with the target market more accurately.

☐ Having built better and closer relationships with the key end customers or the channels to market.

149

☐ Contributing more than 50 per cent of the total benefits set, which the customer pays a premium price for.

☐ The revenue or profit contribution from the collaboration begins to exceed that of the remainder of the parent organization.

COLLABORATION-CENTRIC

Relationship models will change over time, as dictated by market environment, business strategy and partner performance. All movements are relevant within the context of a network organization, but three changes are of particular importance, and of particular significance to the collaboration:

1 An organization which has been a preferred supplier, moves up into a full collaboration relationship.

2 An existing collaborative relationship is now deemed inappropriate. This could either be because that area is no longer seen as strategic, or because partner performance indicates that a different party is needed to achieve the collaboration goals.

3 An existing collaborative relationship is now performing so well, or its contribution is so central to the strategy, that an acquisition or merger is required.

The first of these three situations has been covered in-depth by the first 11 chapters of this book – outlining how to identify, establish and manage such a relationship. We will focus on the other models of evolution for the remainder of this chapter.

Managing downwards

Failure is always a harder process to manage than success. The collaboration has not worked. Either it has not performed, or what was once strategic has now become tactical. How do you break the news? What are the risks of a negative response? Two factors are important to consider:

1 What is the end game of this 'backward' step? Is this the end of the relationship, or a change in relationship model?

2 What is the plan for transition? Relationship changes need to be proactively managed, not allowed to 'drift' towards an alternative model.

The answer to question two depends on the outcome to question one – what is the end game? We need to evaluate this issue, not only based on what we would want it to be, but what is possible. When a marriage breaks up, divorce proceedings are rarely followed by a return to an informal boyfriend-girlfriend relationship. The emotions are not so personal on a corporate tie-up, but the challenge is still there.

Deciding the end game – Reaching a conclusion on the end game requires organizations to consider three levels of evaluation:

1 **Rational** – Based on the strategic contribution made by the current collaborative partner or partners, what type of relationship would provide the best level of support for our organization?

2 **Emotional** – For the key executives involved, how will they feel about this change in relationship? Will some see it as personal failure? Will the ongoing relationship be too difficult to sustain? Will a 'corporate grudge' be held?

3 **Political** – Is this something that would be noticed by either customers or shareholders? Would the breaking up of the collaboration be seen as a signal of low confidence for our organization? The answers to these questions will often depend on the amount of PR coverage invested in the collaboration either at its creation, or since then. Finally, is there a competitive response that this break up could trigger? Would our ex-collaborative partner create something directly with one of our competitors? How much damage could that cause?

Contemplating each of these three elements will enable our organization to close on strategic desire (mostly based on the rational evaluation) and business risk (both emotional and political response). Setting these two against one another, using weighted criteria if it helps to inform the thinking, can provide the basis for reaching a clear end game conclusion. However, now we know where we are going, how do we get there?

Transition plans – A plan is clearly the answer. Who should develop the plan, and what sort of time-scale does it require? This depends on the predicted emotional and political reaction from the current collaborative partner. If the transition is something that the partner would recognize as an appropriate next step, the best model for the transition plan will be to involve both parties. However, if the response is expected to be negative, it will be better to develop the transition plan independently. Discuss contingency options if the ideal time frame to manage the transition is cut short due to the partner's response.

The other key determinant is whether the end game exits the relationship altogether, or drops it down a level in the continuum. If it is the former, there needs to be a parallel 'transition in' plan drawn for whichever organization picks up these activities, or indeed if they are being brought back in-house. If the relationship is moving down a level, the changes are likely to be around governance, contract form and *modus operandi*. In any of these situations, however, the key elements of the transition plan will probably include the following items. For each, indicate the new proposal and the specific changes from the current model.

☐ **Definition of new relationship** – Scope, focus, measures, type and priority.

☐ **Mechanism for relationship management** – Governance, points of interface, key relationship holders, method and frequency of review.

☐ *Modus operandi* – Location, assets, reporting, technology and processes.

☐ **Contractual form** – Model of contract, ownership of assets.

☐ **Communication plan** – For employees, customers and shareholders.

☐ **Contingency plan** – For operational issues or external reactions.

Towards acquisition

In many ways, a collaboration is the ideal stepping stone towards a merger or acquisition. However, study after study shows that around 80 per cent of merger and acquisition activity does not deliver the value needed to justify the premium paid. When these cases are reviewed, common themes emerge to explain why planned value was not realized:

☐ The purchase decision often masks potentially serious differences in perspective on the merger's purpose – between and within both firms.

☐ These differences can persist when paper benefits have not been thought through, in terms of companies underestimating cultural barriers.

☐ Early in the process, when the need and opportunity for action are the highest, critical time is often lost sorting out these issues.

☐ Lack of clear interface management and appropriate level of resources can confound the integration process.

☐ Although original acquisition justifications are always estimates and optimistic, companies often become inflexible and tend to manage the fiction rather than the reality.

☐ Lack of communication between and within the firms is often counter-productive.

☐ Companies underestimate the need to counteract potential value destruction and impact on customers. Companies do not develop operational plans to execute all components of a merger.

☐ Executive leadership and commitment, when needed most, often moves onto the next issue.

☐ The market environment changes during the integration process leading to a change in the key communication messages.

☐ Morale management is over-emphasized during a 'honeymoon' period and then completely forgotten.

☐ Benefit delivery of expected integration savings are not achieved.

All of the issues on this 'lessons learned' list from merger and acquisition failure are addressed as part of the effective creation and management of the collaboration. Success is far more likely if an effective collaboration simply moves up the relationship continuum and the equity swap is made. However, this then poses the fundamental question. Why would you acquire a collaboration which is working well? Do you buy the collaboration, or the other party's parent organization or organizations?

Acquisition tests – Acquisition of a collaboration is only an appropriate way forward in a number of very specific cases. These six tests need to be rigorously applied.

1 The collaboration becomes a competitive risk – BA launched Go as a low-cost operator, which became the darling of investors while BA was going through tough times. Go was put up for sale to remedy the core's problems and was purchased by easyJet, a rival airline. Now Go and easyJet are combined, BA's own child has come back to challenge it head to head in the consumer marketplace. Therefore, collaborative ventures, if highly successful, can suddenly become enormous competitive threats. It is essential to recognize this early enough in order for the collaboration to be purchased before the price premium is too great. In addition, forward thinking should set out how this process will work when the collaboration is initially formed.

2 Collaboration management is poor – As previously mentioned, many of the core concepts of collaboration were originally developed from the Japanese concepts created by the large trading families – the *keiretsu*. Often equity cross-holdings were never more than 1 or 2 per cent, and these huge connected groups of companies were managed through key executive relationships and clear mutual gain. This model fitted well with the cultural norms of Japan. The Western world has struggled with the philosophy because it is more used to command and control models of strategy. Sometimes, a lack of maturity with regard to collaboration approaches means that if a partner is sufficiently strategic, it is better to buy them than attempt to continue operating a relationship model that will not succeed. Firms must build this competence if they are to survive in the new world, yet acceptance of current capability in this area must also prevail.

3 The collaboration encroaches on the strategic core – We have spoken about the two fundamental capabilities that firms cannot give away – their central strategy and strategic architecture, and the ability to manage partners. Over time, successful collaborations that grow and excel can begin to build capability in this area, particularly that of core strategy. Their knowledge of the market, the customers or the core business activities may become so great that they overtake those of the parent. In this instance, acquiring that capability and bringing it back in-house may be the right solution.

4 Another party's strategy changes – When BT's Cellnet (now mm02) was created, it was part owned by Securicor. As the mobile market exploded, the role of BT's mobile division became central to the group's overall strategy. Yet not for Securicor. BT was faced with two choices – to find an alternative way of achieving its strategic aspirations in this area, or to buy Securicor out of their part of this collaboration. It chose the latter, because the original shared strategic need of BT and Securicor no longer reflected BT's purpose for the entity. Its strategy had changed, and with it the deployment of the strategy into Cellnet. The change in strategy also meant that Cellnet was more critical, not less so, for BT to achieve its goal. Cellnet was bought and became BT Cellnet. Less than five years later it was divested by BT in a new organization – mmO2, which again shows the need for relationship models to change as strategies do.

5 Financial engineering is possible – Sometimes the reason for acquisition has nothing to do with strategic changes at all. Plain economics make it a logical thing to do. This may be because of the purchase agreement that was established when the collaboration was formed. It may be that the financial structure of the parent can be enhanced by acquiring the collaboration – either through a new equity vehicle, leveraging debt, or moving assets on or off the balance sheet. When the answer is financial engineering, then the acquisition plan should clearly reflect this issue, not a change in the operational management of the collaboration resources.

6 Legal or regulatory barriers drive it – Finally, legal or regulatory barriers may dictate an acquisition. This is more commonly an issue for 'controlled' industries such as utilities, telecommunications, health or food provision. Either way, trading relationships that are not allowed as business-to-business may be achieved through direct ownership.

We have evaluated the collaboration and concluded that at least one of these six tests has turned up positive – an acquisition appears the right way forward. However, what do we buy – the collaboration, or the other parent companies that originally created the entity?

Who to acquire?

The test defines the answer or at least the preferred model. The test outlines why we wish to acquire the collaboration, rather than carry on as we are. It pinpoints the specific issue where equity ownership provides a competitive advantage for our own organization. From this, the scope of what we would like to acquire, becomes clear. If it is a competitive issue, acquiring the parent organization may be preferable. If it is due to a change in strategic direction of the other parties, acquiring them would be a huge mistake.

As always, desire and the ability to do are sometimes in conflict. Depending on the collaboration model, it may not even exist as a legal entity – the acquisition could be a share exchange, or instead a sale of trading assets only. Either way, the normal rules of valuation will apply and set the boundaries to make this final step on the relationship ladder.

SUMMARY

1   A partnership evolution process requires four basic building blocks to be in place:

    ☐ An agreed relationship continuum.

    ☐ A clear business strategy.

    ☐ A partner management process.

    ☐ The necessary technology infrastructure to run networked businesses.

2   The reality of a relationship can be defined by the buy-sell hierarchy which contains five steps:

    ☐ Step 1 Deliver commodities.

    ☐ Step 2 Deliver 'good' products or services.

    ☐ Step 3 Provide 'good' service and support.

    ☐ Step 4 Contribute to business issues.

    ☐ Step 5 Contribute to organizational issues.

3   The three relationship changes critical to collaborative models are: the move up to a collaboration from a preferred supplier relationship; the move from collaboration to either a lower relationship model or to an exit; or the move from collaboration to acquisition.

4   Movement from a preferred supplier to a collaboration can be achieved using the collaboration establishment process covered in Chapter 6.

5   Changing from a collaboration model to a lesser relationship approach needs to be planned. Consider the rational, emotional and political reactions to the move. In the light of these insights, both the end game and the transition plan can be developed.

6   Where the transition plan indicates that the current partner could have a dramatic reaction, a clear contingency plan is required.

7   Acquiring a collaboration should be considered if one or more of six tests are relevant: the collaboration has become a competitive risk; there is inability to manage a collaborative model; the collaboration has begun to encroach on the strategic core; the other 'parent' organizations have changed their strategy towards the collaboration; there are opportunities to achieve financial engineering through acquisition; or there are legal/regulatory reasons that make it appealing.

8   The test which leads to the acquisition will also guide whether the collaboration should be bought, or the other parent organizations of the collaboration entity.

CHAPTER 14

VERTICAL MONOPOLIES

BEYOND COMPANIES

The fundamental issue for collaborative relationships is that of choice. Who do you choose to approach to be your collaborative partner? And more importantly, what are the implications of this relationship? The issue of implications depends largely on the structure of the industry. If it is a highly fragmented sector with no dominant players, few well-known products, and a widely varying competitive arena as you move from country to country, the implications will be limited. However, this description is inappropriate for most industry sectors. It becomes less relevant as more and more of the major industries consolidate. The mega mergers that have taken place since the 1990s in telecommunications, financial services, life sciences, automotive industry, oil and gas and utilities have already been mentioned. Seemingly huge players have fundamentally changed shape or disappeared as a result of the consolidation machine – Amoco, Mannessman, Airtouch, Orange, Exxon, SmithKline Beecham, Ciba Giegy and Sandoz, to name a few. Even in traditional national industries, for instance, raw material production (coal, steel, aluminium) and retail, consolidation is happening at a rapid pace. As the 'U'-shaped model of industries emerges globally, the issue of choice is increasingly critical.

What happens if the collaborative partner you choose turns out to be a weak player? Have you put all your eggs into one basket and now face a huge competitive disadvantage? By linking up with a collaborative partner, are other opportunities in the industry closed off for you? How do these implications grow as more and more companies link together in a collaborative venture – as a network, not just a collaboration – of business forms? Remember the example of the two airline collaborations – the Star Alliance and OneWorld? Choosing to be a member of one directly implies that you cannot be a member of the other one. However, what if one of the alliances fails? Where does that leave you? Timing is fundamental. Each of these alliances wishes to only have one airline partner that dominates a particular set of routes. That is, after all, the strategic basis for both of them – route sharing and offering customers a single point of access. What happens if you choose the horse you wish to back, but your routes are already sown up by one of your competitors? Do you join the other collaboration believing you are joining the losing party? Or do you try and create a third set of airlines to compete with the existing players? Or have all the big airlines already gone and you are left out in the cold?

These sorts of decisions have absolutely nothing to do with lower unit transaction costs. They do not have much to do with sharing costs along the passenger journey, although the alliance does achieve this. This is a basic question of survival. The focus of the collaborations does not stop at the airline level. As time moves on, these collaborations jointly agree which ticketing technology to use, consolidate spend to agree on fuel partners, even airplane models and so on. And if, instead of 30 organizations each making this decision, there are two collaborative ventures, the impact on the industry supply chain becomes profound. Some big winners and some complete losers emerge. Often, the industry suppliers cannot meet the volume demands of these collaborations, and rapid consolidation is driven, sometimes as the result of the need to meet a single order. In many industries, like oil and gas and retail, driving consolidation of a fragmented supply chain has been an explicit and stated goal of the players dominating the scene. As this process develops, the game has less and less to do with how a particular company operates and meets customer needs. Companies' futures are increasingly decided by the cards they chose to play in the industry game. And the definition of industry is moving. It is not about competitive pressure in the end user marketplace alone. It is also about how choices further up the industry value chain, concerning which group to link with and the implications of doing that, are creating the new paradigm – vertical monopolies.

The automotive industry has probably demonstrated the greatest example of this model, with the powerful car makers, like Ford, General Motors, Audi and BMW, not just requesting suppliers to become sole customer traders, but aligning the rest of the supply market into tiers behind them. They have even moved into direct trading relationships with steel mills and polyolefin suppliers, creating entire vertical chains of companies whose whole futures depend on the success of a single car manufacturer – and in their continued interest in having them as a trading partner. Furthermore, technology then came along to push it to a whole new level. NetMarkets emerged. For the automotive sector, the most well-recognized one was Covisint, a consortium e-market developed by Ford, General Motors and DaimlerChrysler. Suddenly it was not the market power of only one major automotive manufacturer re-profiling the value chain – some of the largest players in the industry were getting together to form a new club. This scenario precisely defines the competitive challenge of the networked industry – the ultimate conclusion of collaborative strategies:

☐ Why would Ford, General Motors and DaimlerChrysler get together – what are the risks and benefits for each of them?

☐ What reaction should the other major automotive players take – should they join Covisint or should three to four of them get together and form a competing collaboration?

☐ How should the supplier community respond to this? Should they choose to join these NetMarkets? Will the major automotive players allow them to join multiple markets? Should they look to defend their position by creating groups of suppliers which form a 'supplier-side' NetMarket?

These questions are not ones of operational improvement or supply chain management. These are fundamental decisions that will shape the power base of industries and the competitive position of every player in them. How these questions are answered will separate those firms that have a future, from those that will not. The arrival of the technology to bring firms together on collaborative trading platforms has been the trigger to a competitive game that has always been there – but the race is now speeding up. Choices have to be taken more rapidly than before; being a bystander and choosing not to play has its own implications. What exactly are the NetMarkets, which are driving the competitive agenda?

A brief history of NetMarkets

The technology, which enables organizations to link together electronically and allows automation to override human intervention, has been around since the early 1980s. Focused on Valued Added Private Networks (VAPNs) and EDI, industries such as automotive and retail are familiar with using networks, and companies like Dell Computers and Cisco have had the mechanism that manages the build to order cycle directly through proprietary systems for some time. Cisco, before the NetMarket concept, directly routed customer orders to its suppliers and, if it was the most cost-effective model, allowed the supplier to ship the product to the end customer directly.

NetMarkets rapidly emerged during the late 1990s, when the internet revolution was in full flow. Trading grounds emerged where multiple suppliers and customers could get together in the digital space and trade without human intervention. There were broadly four types of ownership model:

1 **Direct connection** – Established by a particular company to enable trading with its chosen partners.

2 **Private NetMarkets** – Established by organizations who wished to lead a NetMarket opportunity and create an open trading ground for their suppliers and customers.

3 **Independent NetMarkets** – Established by a third party – often the technology firms – or companies who saw a profitable market opportunity in this area.

4 **Consortium NetMarkets** – Trading places established by major players getting together to create an online presence in an industry.

NetMarkets, like the industries they serve, have being going through their own shakedown. At one point there were as many as 5000 NetMarkets, and the analysts like IDC and Forrester predicted turnover in the trillions. As the internet bubble burst, so did the investment funds. Many NetMarkets realized that the pipedream of collaboration had to be followed up with real delivery capability, which in most cases they did not have. As a result, the number of NetMarkets trading with genuine liquidity has dropped to no more than 200–300 today. Nevertheless, some of these are growing in power and presence, with many breaking the $100 billion mark in trading values. It is increasingly apparent that the consortium NetMarkets – the ones driven by the industry players themselves – are winning. If for no other reason than they bring the trading volumes to give them liquidity and the market power to force the supply community to go online. However, what exactly are they trying to achieve?

TWO DRIVERS OF NETMARKETS

NetMarkets are concerned with bringing new technology to old business challenges. The arrival of the internet as an almost no-cost communication channel, combined with XML as a language which allows 'metadata', rather than specifically defined data structures to be transferred, and intermediaries like WebMethods that allow backward integration, provided the infrastructure necessary to make electronic trading a real possibility. Not a certainty, but at least technically possible. To seize the opportunity presented by this new technology, there has to be an overriding business imperative for the implementation plan. For a two or three company collaboration, often the case in the models described in Chapters 2–5, the 'whole economy' electronic trading platform is not necessary. What additional benefit can result from single collaborative relationships, moving to networks of collaborative relationships, which could, in time, go as far as an entire value chain. There are two – aggregation and integration.

Aggregation – volume and choice

Quite simply, aggregation brings together larger and larger groups of suppliers and customers who can trade together. Many of the well-known exchanges, for example, Covisint, GNX and Chemdex, have essentially focused in this area. Aggregation-based NetMarkets have a stated benefit for both the buy-side and sell-side companies:

☐ For buy-side companies, the ability to aggregate procurement spend together drives lower unit costs in return for volume.

☐ On the sell-side, bringing together larger trading groups provides new potential customers for suppliers, enabling growth as a result of participation.

That is the theory. Naturally, operational reality has shown, in most cases, a slightly different dynamic. The buyers have indeed been able to pool the purchasing power and hammer down the unit purchase price. However, buyers have only felt comfortable doing this in commodity areas that do not differentiate their end-use products or services. Which is why, even in industries where NetMarkets are well developed, major players do not purchase more than 10–15 per cent of their spend in this way. And as for the suppliers, there is the potential of finding new customers. However, in general, aggregation-based NetMarkets carry concerns about trading with partners you do not know, where off-line trust has not been established. For most firms that barrier is high enough to focus trading on known players. When Toyota, who operates a proprietary trading system with its small group of collaborative partners, was asked to join Covisint, it politely accepted for non-core commodity based items. Nevertheless, it decided to deal with core commodities using current practice. After all, price was not the primary issue in its collaborative relationships and when all is said and done, price seems to be the main focus for aggregation NetMarkets to date.

Integration – alignment and commonality

Integration is a wholly different key driver. This is more about the flow of information between organization and the accessibility of common business processes for all. At the lowest level, NetMarkets, which have focused on integration have created common procurement processes, allowing the ease and speed of Request for Quotation (RFQ)-based processes to dramatically improve. When information is shared along the order to deliver cycle, inventory levels within an industry supply chain can reduce, as safety stocks at each organizational boundary are lowered to a single safety level for all parties. Moreover, as this level of integration improves, sales growth, improved fulfilment rates, shared new product development and R&D are all potential next steps. Toyota, Cisco and Dell Computers are examples that fit into this example. Although, in common they are all private NetMarkets. This is partly because the level of off-line cultural alignment, creation of shared goals and trust needed to operate in this manner, may be enabled by technology, but technology cannot drive its creation.

Collaboration – aggregation and integration

In broad terms, today's public NetMarkets offer high aggregation benefits and little in terms of integration. Private NetMarkets offer the reverse, with high integration benefits and little in terms of aggregation. The two airline collaborations can offer illustration. The NetMarket that would realize the true benefits of these groups of partners would be one that allows complete integration of business process across the organizations and their supplying partners, as well as aggregation of spend back down the value chain. In other words, a collaborative NetMarket infrastructure to support a vertical monopoly.

It is probably fair to conclude that no such NetMarket exists today. Firms struggle to trust suppliers on whom they are mutually dependent – trusting competitors is unsurprisingly a difficult bridge to cross. However, most of these NetMarkets are still in their formative stages and their futures will be watched with interest by many.

It is evident that two types of owners drive collaborative NetMarkets. Private owners and consortium. The private NetMarkets are owned by a particular firm, often a dominant player. These firms fund the investment to bring their key suppliers and customers into a collaborative arrangement, hoping this will tie them to a future of mutual success. Private NetMarkets benefit from speed of decision making, but the challenge of liquidity. The consortium NetMarkets are where the real industry power games are played.

THE IMPLEMENTATION BARRIERS

Creating collaborative operations between two organizations can prove challenging. When you are trying to meld ten or 20 firms into a fully connected network of trading partners, focused on mutual success, the implementation hurdles can be high. Four problems are discernible: common standards, technology integration, confidentiality and choice.

Common standards

Managing to get all of the functions within a single firm together, to agree common standards, has its challenges. Achieving this across companies is even harder. To create this single, common and open trading platform there needs to be a consistent approach to how data is defined and information collected. Products need a common code or identifier. Yet probably each firm has developed their own nomenclature based on historical decisions. What defines a claim, a delivery location or even a customer? It is not only data definitions – technology standards, particularly for XML language, dictate how these protocols are turned into operational reality. Jeff Stamen, the CEO of Syncra Systems who provide Collaborative Planning, Forecasting and Replenishment (CPFR) tools, believes that if product and process standards could be agreed in the US retail industry, savings of 20 per cent in total value chain costs could be achieved[1].

Technology integration

Many NetMarkets have turned out be nothing more than a misleading front-end interface. Once an order is placed by one party, that information is sent at internet speed to the supplying firm, who promptly print out the order and re-key it into their back-end transaction systems. When the order is ready, the supplier keys in that information to the NetMarket interface, which sends it, again at lightning internet speed to the customer, who also prints it out and keys it into their system. Not exactly transformational collaborative technology. Obviously, this lack of integration adds cost to the process, because human intervention, not technological automation drives transaction. However, it also inhibits the true potential of collaboration. For integrated planning and operations to be possible, customers need to see inside suppliers' systems to view what is 'available to promise'. The status of trucks which are

[1] *A–Z of eHeroes*, written and researched by Suntop Media, Capstone.

on route, delivering finished products, should be available to all parties, not just the supplying organization. To achieve this enabling integration is not about melding front office systems together, it is about a fundamental integration of Enterprise Resource Planning (ERP) and collaborative tools, to create a single technology platform.

Confidentiality

Who exactly should be able to see what? Do we understand our systems enough to execute the decided security protocols? There are many examples of firms who first implemented ERP packages, only to find that the chief executive's salary was on open display, or the cost of the new head office building. Enabling a single point of access to all data, through integration technology, carries the challenge of being able to shut off all routes to those who should not see them. Sometimes these security protocols are based around legal requirements, for instance, data protection and individual confidentiality agreements with particular customers or suppliers. For others, it is more about protecting competitive information. This is particularly pertinent when NetMarket systems give partial access to others along the relationship continuum, not just to collaborative partners, in order for a full networked world to be created.

Choice

Finally, who chooses? Who decides that a new player can join the game? Are there levels of membership? As these vertical monopolies emerge, what is the decision-making process? Who decides if a new airline can join the Star Alliance? What are the entry criteria if BMW wanted to take a lead position within Corvisint? Do all the entry tickets carry the same level of access? Having a clear process and set of rules is important, but increasingly it will be industry power, not a rule book, that will define the answers. Rules, after all, tend to be made by those in authority to make them. In the commercial sphere, market power, not democratic votes, dictates who has authority.

MAKING CHOICES – THE INDUSTRY STRATEGY

This leads us back to the critical questions. How do you make your choices? Do you go private or consortium for NetMarkets? Do you join someone else's or do you lead? Who do you want on board, and how do you predict the responses of others in the chain? Is it more important to focus on the competitors in your step of the value chain, or to try and tie up the players further down the chain? Three factors help to answer these questions, which differ for each organization:

1 What is the level of industry consolidation?

2 How stand-alone is the product or service?

3 What is your organization's current competitive position?

We can take Wal-Mart as an example. Suppose that the major retailers wish to get together to initially drive aggregation down the value chain. A consortium NetMarket is required. What should Wal-Mart do? The industry is at a high level of consolidation, the products in question are highly definable, but Wal-Mart is currently the strongest player. It has the greatest differentiation in terms of market and purchasing power. Getting Wal-Mart into your consortium NetMarket is good for all the other players – yet the direct result for Wal-Mart is a reduction in the competitive gap it has over its key competitors. Thus, choosing not to play would seem the better choice. Wal-Mart is in a much stronger position to drive a private NetMarket than participate in a consortium model. The firm will gain its value from sowing further up the value chain behind it, rather than letting its current market power be dispersed across its competitors.

We are in the formative stages for NetMarkets, and so an industry strategy at this point can favour multiple routes. The Dow Chemical Company is a case in point. For suppliers critical to its own core business, and where collaborative relationships are the chosen path, Dow uses a private NetMarket mechanism. Integration, not aggregation is key here. For other purchases that are non-core, Dow uses a variety of NetMarkets, depending on the type of item being procured, and focuses more on aggregation. Traderanger, the consortium NetMarket developed by most of the major industry players, is used, as is SciQuest for laboratory supplies and Zone Trader for disposal of excess equipment. Dow also participates in ChemConnect, an independent NetMarket but one in which it holds an equity stake, as a source of new potential opportunities. Finally, Dow uses its own e-mart NetMarket to focus on indirects, particularly where auctioning can be used.

On the sales side, Dow's dominant market position means that it prefers to deal directly with its key customers through MyAccount@Dow. Where customers are looking to aggregate, however, Dow participates on the consortium NetMarkets of Omnexus and Elemica. As the need for both integration and aggregation move forward, Elemica increasingly focuses on gaining ERP integration in this front-office trading tool. Finally, where Dow has volumes that it simply wishes to shift at spot prices, then ChemConnect can be used.

Dow is one example of an organization choosing where to drive the agenda, where to participate and where to opt out. A similar picture can be drawn for many other players.

A framework for decisions

The tangible outcomes of the options of industry consolidation, stand-alone products or services and current competitive strength are investment choices. Do you spend $20 million creating a private NetMarket for you and your current eight collaborative ventures? Do you pay the $5 million it will take to integrate your SAP system into a consortium NetMarket?

STRENGTH OF ACTIONS REQUIRED

		Low urgency	CONTINUUM		High urgency

STRATEGIC POSITION	AGGRESSIVE OR OPPORTUNISTIC	☐ Revenue expectations ☐ Payback period (ROI) ☐ Cashflow implications ☐ Product or service fit	☐ Organizational structure ☐ Financial strength ☐ Investor expectations ☐ Strategic fit with existing offering
	DEFENSIVE	☐ Net revenue shift ☐ Investor expectations ☐ Profit implications ☐ Alternative investment opportunities	☐ Revenue at risk ☐ Financial strength ☐ Alternative revenue potential ☐ Competitor actions

ECONOMIC-BASED ⟶ STRATEGIC-BASED

TABLE 14.1: Investment criteria for vertical monopolies

Should you take a $50 million equity stake in a new independent NetMarket that is being established? Do you drive the agenda for industry regulations of standards? Investment criteria is the most powerful model to understand the real decisions to be made. Two factors should be considered:

1 Am I taking a defensive or aggressive position? Am I driving the action or am I being forced into a decision because others in the industry have made a move that I need to respond to?

2 Is this an economic-based decision or a strategic one? Can I define the ROI due to aggregation benefits, or am I taking a strategic 'punt' because this is a potential survival issue?

On this four box matrix, the defensive (I don't have a choice) and economic (I can see the return) decisions are the easiest ones to make. In many ways being in a defensive decision making mode is a sign of failure in its own right. Proactive actions were not taken when real choice was available, and now external factors have all but removed the options. However, it is the strategic based aggressive quadrant where industry winners are made, but also the zone where hard facts and data are least available.

SUMMARY

1 The philosophy of collaboration has reached a new level with the emergence of NetMarkets, which operate at the industry level.

2 There are four main ownership models for NetMarkets: direct, private, independent and consortium.

3 NetMarkets are currently going through a shakedown, with the 5000 start ups reducing to 200–300 major trading entities.

4 Two drivers define the benefits of NetMarkets – aggregation and integration.

5 Aggregation allows for increased purchasing power and new sales opportunities, but struggles outside commodity products and services and where trust-based relationships are needed.

6 Integration has mostly happened in direct trading relationships, where significant off-line work has been done. These are typically traditional collaborative relationships.

7 Industry collaboration, and the emergence of vertical monopolies, is happening when both aggregation and integration is brought together in a single industry model.

8 Implementation of these models proves challenging due to the difficulties of agreeing common standards, technology integration, confidentiality and choice.

9 Choosing a strategy at the industry level is defined by three criteria: the level of industry consolidation, the stand-alone nature of the products or services and the current competitive position of the organization.

10 The industry landscape is currently emerging for most sectors, and firms have to choose which routes to follow.

11 Investment decisions need to be guided by whether an option is aggressive or defensive, and whether the basis of the move is an economic or strategic one.

12 The greatest opportunity will be realized when firms make aggressive strategy-based investment decisions. These also carry with them the highest risk factor.

CONCLUSION

PUTTING IT ALL TOGETHER

Collaboration has become one of the most significant business ideologies of the twenty-first century. The firms of the new world, like Microsoft, Cisco, Intel and Vodafone, have developed from almost start up operations, to become some of the most dominant forces in global commerce, in just a decade. One can argue about whether this was achieved by luck, judgement or some strong competitive strategies, but the achievements cannot be disputed. The common theme is that these firms did not try and do it alone. They created strategic collaborations in order to scale at speed and to dominate geographical and product markets in steps, not incrementally. Moreover, if it was a more efficient or effective model, they relied on other firms' expertise to get them there. The companies all had one thing in their favour – they had 'marketplace currency'. They were firms who everyone wanted to partner. They were seen as the creators of the new age.

Increasingly, as technology connects the trading world, restrictive legislation gradually disappears, and as the workforce becomes ever more mobile, it will be our collaborative partners, as much as our customer service, that will define the future. This book has attempted to provide a framework for organizations grappling with the collaboration dilemma, and to give tools, approaches and examples of how to respond. Nevertheless, in the competitive landscape, the collaboration game is only just beginning. The bets are being placed, but for most industries, the roulette wheel has not yet begun to spin. There are four questions to consider when entering the collaboration game, and this book has laid out the route map for you:

The key collaboration questions

1 When should you collaborate?

2 How do you choose which collaboration model to use?

3 How do you realize the expected value from the collaboration?

4 With the arrival of the digital economy, how do you manage collaborative relationships at the industry level in this increasingly networked world?

The following points summarize the key messages made throughout this book.

When should you collaborate?

Collaborative relationships are by their very definition strategic. These relationships sit below the equity integration of two firms – whether through merger or acquisition. Therefore, the only elements of delivery that an organization should consider for this model of business-to-business relationship are those that make a material contribution to the strategic aims of the enterprise.

However, being strategic is not sufficient in its own right. For collaboration to be an appropriate model, there must be a suitable external organization with greater resources, capabilities or market power and who could enable that business goal to be delivered more easily. In summary, the need for collaboration must pass two tests:

1   The organization has a **strategic need**.

2   There is at least one **external organization** with the ability to meet that need **faster, better or cheaper** than the organization with the strategic need.

How do you choose which collaboration model to use?

The strategic need leads to different types of requirements for prospective collaborative parties. Collaborations need to be considered in a similar manner to projects. They exist for a singular and focused purpose. Their scope can be defined, as can their strategic objectives. Four collaboration models are highlighted in this book, which exist to plug different strategic gaps. While possible for a single business-to-business relationship to attempt to operate more than one of these models – this needs to be recognized as two separate collaborative efforts that happen to involve the same companies. It is not one collaborative endeavour. There is a fifth model of collaboration we have not discussed, which is where the preferred relationship model is one of merger, but for reasons of either legal, regulatory or operational constraint this cannot be the case. In this instance, a full integration process would happen; this is not the collaboration approach under normal circumstances.

The four areas of strategic need, and the collaboration model appropriate to fulfil that need are as follows:

1   Where organizations are looking for a partner to operate a business process or processes that are core (i.e. strategic), then a **supply chain collaboration** model is appropriate.

2   If the strategic gap is one of skills, competence or technological know-how, a **capability-based collaboration** model is required.

3   When two or more organizations wish to bring a new customer offering to the marketplace, which demands resources of more than one organization to make it a commercial reality, a **proposition-based collaboration** will deliver.

4   Where greater market dominance can be achieved for existing products or services by capitalizing on a channel to market which another organization has control over, then raw Porterian power can be exerted through a **competitive collaboration.**

How do you realize the expected value from the collaboration?

Regardless of the collaboration model appropriate to your firm's specific strategic needs, the process by which effective collaborative ventures are created follows a common path – the collaboration establishment process. Collaboration success follows five clearly demarcated phases:

1   Evaluating the **business case**, both independently and collectively for the collaboration.

2   Taking part in **transformation design and planning**.

3 Conducting joint **implementation planning**, which will take aspired goals into operational reality.

4 **Implementing** the shared plan through key deployment levers.

5 **Evaluating results** of the collaboration against its original business case expectations and driving improvement.

Throughout the process of collaboration establishment, as well as the ongoing management and monitoring of the collaboration, there are four critical factors to ensure success:

1 Conducting a rigorous process upfront for collaborative **partner selection**. Never allow existing relationships to be a factor in defining a collaborative partner but instead focus on:

☐ Agreeing design intent.

☐ Developing a gate-based process.

☐ Only having one company on the final short list.

2 Focus on achieving **shared goals and values** between the collaborative partners. This is both at a strategic level, but also monitored in terms of operational realization of aspired outcomes. It can be achieved by:

☐ Adopting the framework of vision, mission and values.

☐ Using parallel descriptors to understand relative perceptions.

☐ Taking real life scenarios to test the goals and values.

3 Operate an **integrated planning process**, not only when the collaboration is initiated, but as an ongoing mechanism. Use the process to manage the end-to-end systems of the collaboration and to share common information through the governance structure of the entity by:

☐ Linking objectives to organizational roles.

☐ Balancing incremental and step-change opportunities.

☐ Aligning the plan to measures.

4 Underpin the collaboration with a single, consistent and shared **measurement model**. Base a Plan-Do-Review for **performance management** around this. Ensure that all parties view the same information, in the same manner, against agreed performance standard for the collaboration to operate in an aligned manner. This can be achieved by:

☐ Linking top level measures to operational activities.

☐ Using Portal technology to unify data and deliver consistency.

☐ Including knowledge management in the scope of the model.

With the arrival of the digital economy, how do you manage collaborative relationships at the industry level in this increasingly networked world?

Collaborative technology tools have opened up new possibilities to realize the vision of joined up organizations. More significantly, they have painted a picture for the ultimate prize – a fully networked industry. Companies operating from the same enabling platform, sharing common standards and protocols, removing the non-added value costs at the organizational interface, and flowing customer orders back up the industry value chain to raw material providers. However, this simplistic and, perhaps idealistic model of the future, ignores the intense competitive dynamic in industries continuing to consolidate, globalizing further, and who are blurring their boundaries with one another.

Choosing a way forward in the digital economy needs to go beyond opportunities for reduced inventory, lower transaction costs and reduced unit purchasing power. The critical decisions relate to which industry collaboration your firm should participate in, the consequences of doing so, and if aggressive actions should be taken to move the agenda forward. Being ready to play in the networked economy necessitates five precursors:

1 Absolute clarity and internal capability to manage the strategy of the organization. Knowing what is core, and translating that strategy into market, process and organizational strategies, underpinned by performance measures that can govern the way third-party relationships are managed.

2 A model for different types of business-to-business relationships, which the firm operates, from 'spot' suppliers through to full collaborative partners.

3 Knowing the operational implications of how each relationship type is managed, plugged into the network and the level of information sharing and integration which takes place.

4 The competence and process for managing partners along this relationship continuum, both upwards and downwards as strategic need and partner performance change.

5 An ability to evaluate customer, supplier and competitor reactions to choices that the networked economy brings, particularly in relation to value chain collaboration.

With these precursors in place, increased networking in the economy offers benefits of aggregation and integration. NetMarkets are the vehicle through which most of these benefits are offered – whether direct, private, independent or consortium. Choosing an appropriate direction in what is still a forming landscape, is based on three factors:

1 The level of **consolidation** in the industry.

2 The degree to which the industries' products and services are **stand-alone**.

3 The current **competitive power** of your organization.

These choices are ultimately investment decisions. Whether for internal projects, equity investments in new entities, or contributions towards external industry initiatives. How to consider these investments will depend on two criteria:

1 The degree to which the investment is considered as a defensive action, versus an aggressive or opportunistic move.

2 The degree to which the investment is made due to the existence of a clear economic business case, rather than a strategic move to position the firm for the long term.

CLOSING THOUGHTS

Since the early 1990s, early concepts of partnering and alliancing have been catapulted into the front line of commercial success. The new world giants build their kingdoms with effective collaborative relationships. As firms recognize that the resources base of other organizations can be accessed without purchasing them, the traditional barriers to expansion are lifted. New players are becoming global giants without building, making or owning any part of their operations.

New trading grounds have emerged with the arrival of the digital economy. The collaborative NetMarkets. Some have already fallen by the wayside, but others grow from strength to strength. This is the time to make long-term strategic choices with the slimmest of information and facts. Standing by while others make their choices is not an option. The landscape of this increasing global, consolidating and connected corporate world is forming. Choices bring with them risks, implications and consequences. What choices will your organization make in this landscape?